Hunting the German Shark

The Author

Hunting the German Shark

The U.S. Navy and the German U-Boat Threat
During the First World War

Herman Whitaker

LEONAUR

Hunting the German Shark
The U.S. Navy and the German U-Boat Threat
During the First World War
by Herman Whitaker

First published under the title
Hunting the German Shark

Leonaur is an imprint of Oakpast Ltd

Copyright in this form © 2011 Oakpast Ltd

ISBN: 978-0-85706-645-9 (hardcover)
ISBN: 978-0-85706-646-6 (softcover)

http://www.leonaur.com

Contents

To Vice Admiral William Sowden Sims
And His Command.
The Officers and Men of the American Naval Forces
in European Waters,
This Book
is Dedicated by Their Shipmate,
The Author

CHAPTER 1

The American Naval Forces in European Waters

It is now more than a year since, (as at time of first publication), the first units of the American Fleet sailed away from our shores and were promptly lost to view in those mists of secrecy with which the British Admiralty then camouflaged its sea operations. Now and then a flash of information blazed out of the war fogs—as when the British First Sea Lord announced in Parliament early in 1918 that "between forty and fifty *per cent*, of U-boats were being sunk." But of the manner in which they came to their ends we were not informed.

Generally speaking, that policy of silence was good at the time, though it was not good for the Hun, who never could find out what became of those of his U-boats that failed to return to port. Whether they were sunk by shell-fire, mines, torpedo, collision with each other or with sunken rocks, or through internal defects of their own, he could not tell. He knew only that after two and a half voyages, on the average, they did not return; and we have good reason to know that the mystery that surrounded their fate seriously impaired the morale of his crews.

For England—a small country geographically, and the seat of the underseas—war this policy of silence did not entail much hardship. Considerable news seeps down to the man in the street from clubs and other sources. Though nothing was printed of the submarine war, everybody knew that it was going well: news of individual feats of gallantry soon spread through the nation.

In America, however, the conditions are entirely different. San Francisco is farther from New York than the latter city is from London. We are too far from the war, our borders are too wide, for the dissemination of information by word of mouth. After our fleet sailed away, it might, for anything we knew to the contrary, have gone straight to the bottom. Not till the developments of the underseas war permitted a relaxation in the rule of silence, eight months later, did we hear anything of it. The wise policy of publicity within certain bounds that followed permitted the writing of the following chapters on the work of the American Fleet.

The account of its disposition and operations may well begin with a glance at the situation that the first units found on their arrival in British waters in 1917. For the last two days of the voyage they cruised amid the wreckage of torpedoed ships—boxes, barrels, crates; smashed boats, often with dead and dying men in them; drowned animals; alas! far too often, dead men and women, still upheld by life-preservers.

Far better, however, than by any pen picture, the situation is set forth in the accompanying map, which approximately gives the sinkings of Allied ships in April, 1917. Each of the black dots and circles that surround the Allied coasts with a mourning border represents a ship sunk by torpedo, mine, or gunfire. But, one year later, the month of April showed a happy reduction in sinkings of 70 *per cent.*

This striking change appears still more remarkable when we remember the tremendous volume of transport tonnage that was added to the normal merchant trade during the year. Troop-and supply-ships aggregating two and a quarter millions of tons streamed in a gigantic ferry across the Atlantic, carrying a million American soldiers to France. These ships had to be and were securely convoyed,—so securely that even Hindenburg acknowledged that it was suicide for a U-boat to attack them, and this extra service drew from the English and American fleets a large number of destroyers that would otherwise have been used to protect merchant shipping and hunt down U-boats. It goes without saying, therefore, that but for this paramount necessity, the number of merchant sinkings would have been still less; the number of U-boats sunks, still more.

As it is we may rest satisfied; for the most gratifying feature is found in the fact that in the months of February, March, and April, 1918, the two great curves that represent U-boats sunk and new ships built showed a remarkable acceleration. In the first year of the war the U-boat curve was little better than horizontal. It really began to curve late in the following year, and has gone on bending upwards more and more steeply, until, in the last few months, it threatens to become vertical.

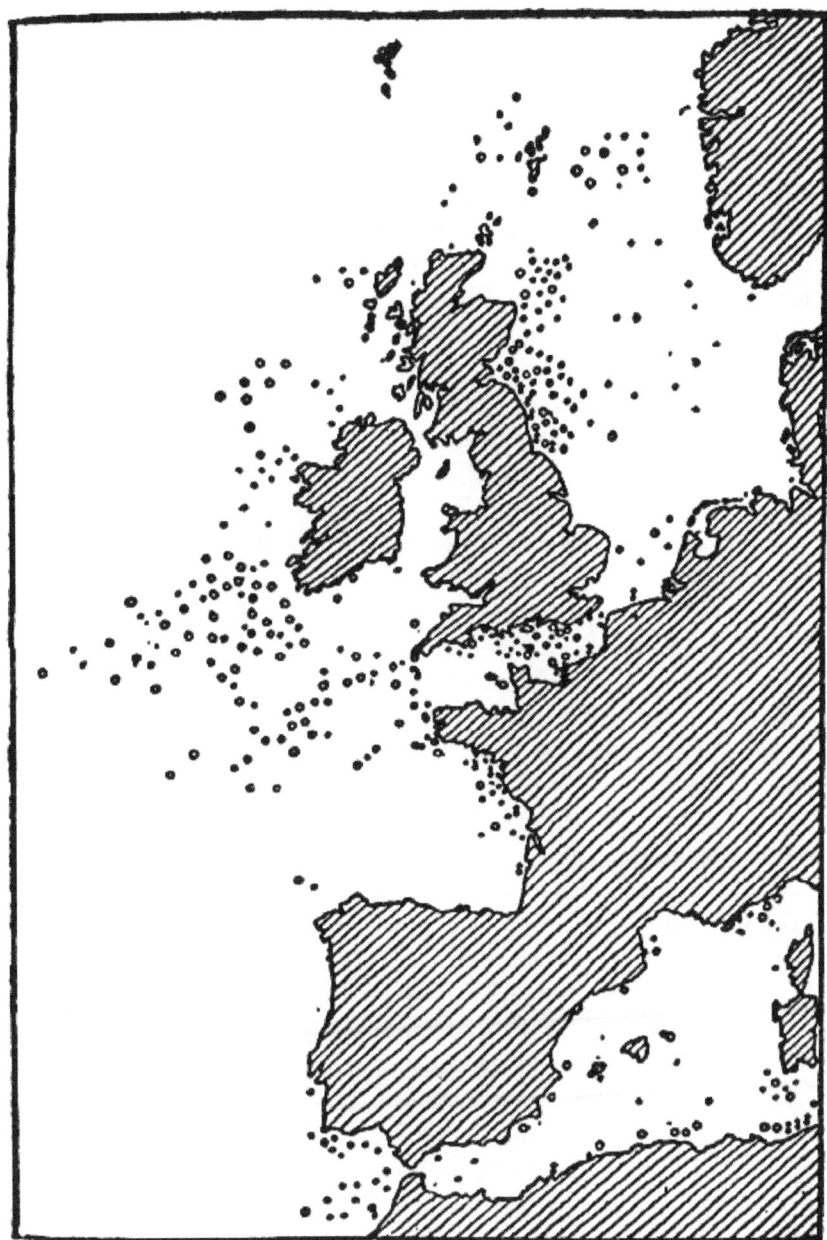

We are now (September, 1918) sinking U-boats faster than the Germans can build them. We are building ships far faster than the U-boats can sink them. In the sense of a contest in which the issue is still at stake, the underseas war is over. Henceforth it descends to the level of privateering and sporadic raids, which will become fewer as the months go by.

This remarkable showing is, of course, the product of many factors—the introduction and extension of the convoy system; improved methods of hunting U-boats by depth-mine barrages; the perfection of listening devices; the use of Allied submarines to hunt down U-boats; the extension of the Naval Aviation Service, both American and English; the closing of Zeebrügge and Ostend and the blocking of other U-boat routes by new minefields: in all of which the American Fleet has done good work.

The American Fleet is made up of a composition of battleships, dreadnoughts, destroyers, scout-cruisers, submarines, armed yachts, coastguard vessels, mine-layers, and repair ships, manned by a personnel of more than forty thousand men. To this now has to be added over a hundred "chasers" and their crews; many thousands of men serving on troop-and supply-ships, naval transports, as armed guards; radio and signal men; naval gun crews furnished to merchant vessels; lastly, ten thousand men of the American Naval Aviation Service. Lumping them all together, a hundred thousand men would be a conservative estimate of the American naval forces, either serving directly under the command of Admiral Sims or coming and going in the transport service.

Judged by any standard, this is a large fleet, and one of the most satisfactory things about it—to an American, at least—is found in the fact that its upkeep has laid no additional burden on England, already over-weighted with her own war costs and those of weaker allies. Our fleet is practically self-sustaining.

All its food and supplies have been sent by the United States. Excepting major operations that require a dry-dock, it makes its own repairs. It manufactures its own torpedoes; provides its own hospitals; and as sailors, like other men, cannot live by bread alone, it has established numerous recreation buildings, with cinema theatres, dormitories, dining, reading, writing, and bath rooms, the quality of which may be gaged from the fact that one single establishment cost thirty thousand dollars.

For convenience in operations, the fleet is divided into five principal units. The first to go over, a flotilla of crack destroyers, operated in Irish waters, and made good in both offensive and defensive warfare against the submarines. Two vessels of this flotilla steamed sixty-four thousand miles apiece during the year—a distance equal to a voyage from Liverpool to New York and return—each month. Thirty of them steamed one million five hundred thousand miles on convoy duty.

The record of the armed yachts and destroyers in French waters is equally good. In conjunction with the French and English fleets and their sister flotilla in Irish waters, they have handled the American transport trade, also many coastal convoys, with a remarkably small loss in sinkings.

Credit for this has to be shared with the American Naval Aviation Service, which has established many stations in France. For there is nothing the U-boat dreads more than the sea-planes—great hawks of the sea, which come booming out from the land to find and strike their steel prey.

This service also operates some stations in England, Ireland, and Italy. Some of its men were in the big seaplane fight in Heligoland Bight, when nine Allied planes engaged seventeen Huns. Others have fought frequent engagements. Summing the naval air service, one may say that its work is invaluable.

A third American division operates in the Mediterranean—under severe handicaps, for the geographical features of that long and narrow sea render it an ideal ground for U-boat operations. Operating from their bases at Pola and Cattaro, on the Adriatic Sea, the U-boats get two fine chances, coming and going, at every ship. The neutrality of Spain is also in their favour, providing a city of refuge to which they can fly when hard pressed or too badly damaged to keep the seas. In spite, however, of these handicaps, sinkings in the Mediterranean have been cut down sixty-five *per cent*, during the year.

Next come the submarines, two units of which operate on bases wide apart. One holds a group of islands, which might otherwise serve as a U-boat base, while the other actively hunts them through British waters. Their work is extremely valuable, for it has increased the hardships of Hun U-boat life several hundred *per cent*. Thanks to the Allied submarines, Fritz can no longer bask in the sunlight till the masts of a convoy poke up from behind the horizon; for he never knows when a torpedo may land on his solar plexus.

Having taken an eight-day cruise in an American submarine, I am in a position to know exactly what prolonged submergence means.

Fritz's life—never a happy one—has through the operations of Allied submarines become in-supportable. Dogged by patrols, bombed by seaplanes, voyaging always through a maze of nets and mines, he is now hunted underseas by huge steel sharks of his own kind.

Lastly, a battleship division operates with the British Grand Fleet in the North Sea, assisting in the work of keeping the German High Seas Fleet bottled up in harbour. While cruising recently, this division narrowly missed contact with the enemy, and the disappointment of the entire personnel thereat is beyond my power in words. Now they are hungering for another real chance at the Hun.

This, then, briefly sums the disposition and operations for a year of the American Fleet. Space does not permit description of the real hardships and dangers of the work. In! Coal up! Out! describes the life. Blow high, blow low, it ran its convoys to break the strangler's cord of U-boats and keep the stream of ships in circulation.

This was not accomplished without a price in lives. The armed yacht *Alcedo*, torpedoed in French waters; the *Jacob Jones*, sunk in the Channel; the *Chauncey*, rammed and sunk during a fog—these, with a hundred of their crews and twenty-two other lads washed off the decks of destroyers during night storms, are the price the American Navy has paid for the safe delivery of Allied supplies. But that was inevitable. Having done its duty according to its lights, the fleet asks no higher praise than that freely accorded by the man—who next to its own Admiral Sims—knows it better than any other man alive, Admiral Sir Lewis Bayley, Commander-in-Chief of the American flotilla in Irish waters:

I want to express my deep gratitude to the United States officers and ratings for the skill, energy, and unfailing good nature which they have constantly shown; qualities that have materially assisted the war by enabling the ships of the Allied Powers to cross the ocean in comparative freedom.

To command you is an honour; to work with you a pleasure; to know you is to know the best traits of the Anglo-Saxon people.

CHAPTER 2

"Sim's Circus, Continuous!"

When Admiral Sims granted my request to visit the destroyer flotilla in Irish waters, his eyes took on a twinkle that I was destined to see again—in the eyes of the British base Admiral, to whom I reported two days later, in those of the chief of staff of the American flotilla; also those of the commander in whose vessel I finally went out. His executive officer even laughed—and apologized. They all asked, quite casually, how much of a sailor I was, and gave non-committal nods to tales of voyages on big ships. Then they all twinkled again.

From the train window approaching the base I obtained my first view of "Sims's circus," as the flotilla has been named by an irreverent ensign. At least, I obtained my first astonished view of the minor portion thereof that chanced to be in port. For the base Admiral is a most efficient man. His offices and house windows both overlook the water, and it's said by our skippers that his idea of heaven is "a harbour clear of ships and every destroyer at sea."

I may add from personal observation that never was there a man who did so much to make his idea of heaven obtain on earth. Nothing short of a "salty condenser" will procure from him a stay in port—which reminds me of a question put by a green ensign in our wardroom one day:

"Is the water we drink pure enough to use in our boilers?"

To which was given in indignant chorus: "Of course not! What do you think you are?"

Returning again to the flotilla. A convoy was ready to sail; a dozen or so of our destroyers were to be seen nestling like speckled chickens under the wings of the mother repair ships.

I said "speckled." It is, however, too weak a term for the "dazzle" paint with which they were bedaubed. No wonder the irreverent ensign dubbed them the "circus."

Barred, striped, blotched, smudged, ring-streaked with vivid pinks, arsenic greens, blowsy reds, violent blues, they looked like—like—like nothing in the world unless it be that most poisonous of drinks, a *'Frisco pousse café*. All of the giraffes, zebras, leopards, and tigers ever assembled in the "World's Greatest Aggregation" exhibit conventional patterns in comparison with this destroyer camouflage. The exception to this blazing colour scheme, a recent arrival from home, looked, in her dull lead paint, like a Puritan maiden that had fallen by accident into a blowsy company of painted Jezebels. The object of this wanton display is, of course, to fool Fritz of the submarines. That it might do so by hurting his eyes or the shock to his artistic sensibilities none would deny; but I found it hard to believe that these rainbow colours make a difference in visibility. Yet they do. Whereas at sea the following day, the Puritan maiden showed a clear black outline at four miles with every spar clearly defined, the Jezebels presented at the same distance a blurred, wavering mass of colour. It was difficult to tell bow from stern or judge their direction. They presented about as fair a target as does a darting hummingbird.

The vessel I went out on had struck America's first blow in the war by attacking one of the submarines that opposed our transports in the Atlantic. The thought was hot in my mind when, after boarding her, my eye wandered from the knifelike bows back over the shotted guns, grim torpedo tubes, along the low, rakish hull to the stern, where two depth-mines hung poised for instant use.

Of all the enginery of destruction produced in the war, there is no weapon more terrible than these. The explosion of one lifts a column of water thirty yards wide fifty feet above the sea. One that was discharged nearly two hundred yards away from a 30,000-ton ocean liner heaved her up six inches in the water. So terrible are they that destroyers drop them only when running at high speed to insure a "get-away," and even then the iron floor-plates of the boiler-room are often lifted by the concussion.

From the bridge I watched this slender arrow of a ship slip out through the harbour headlands, where a number of other destroyers were at work combing the offing for submarines before the convoy came out. They were beautiful to see—shooting like a school of rainbow flying-fish over the long green seas; careening on swift turns, laying the white lace of their wakes over sixty square miles of sea. Among them, graceful as a swallow, was the *Jacob Jones*, the unfortunate vessel which, torpedoed two weeks later, now lies with sixty-four of our brave lads at the bottom of the sea. It is only necessary to record that she did not die unavenged.

Were I permitted to tell the number of sinkings to the credit of our fleet, it would cause surprise. I may say that dozens of submarines are strewn over the ocean floor around the British Isles. Out of the five sinkings that Mr. Lloyd-George was to announce in Parliament that very night as being the bag for one day, two were to the credit of our base.

CHAPTER 3

Capturing a U-Boat

I heard the stories of some of those submarines while we were circling and swooping above them.

"You see that marker?" The executive officer on the bridge indicated a small buoy as we swept by. "There was something funny about the way that fellow got his.

"A little patrol-boat happened to cross his wake. Cheeky little beggars, those patrols. Though he had nothing but an old-style depth-charge, he took a chance, dropped it at the head of the wake, then listened around.

"After a while he heard calking hammers going on the bottom, and knew that Fritz was down there making repairs. So he sent out a radio, and a destroyer came up and dropped a big charge of TNT squarely on top of Fritz. His oil came up in gushes, and a diver found him lying on his side, like a dead whale next day, split wide open, like a gutted fish.

"There's another lying some miles away over there. The British Admiralty has to be shown before it gives credit for a sinking, and, though oil came up in gushes after we dropped the 'ash-can,'"—thus does the American sailor irreverently allude to the depth-mine,— "they gave us no credit till another skipper reported the sea covered with oil two days later in the same place.

"Even then they only allowed us a probable sinking. But it is all right. Fritz is cunning; will often pump out a little oil when we drop a charge to make us think we've got his goat."

While he was talking there had been no let up in the combing of the offing for submarines. Here and there, back and forth, the destroyers swooped with birdlike circlings, and no words can describe the thoroughness of the watch upon the sea. From the bridge by officers and quartermasters, by the men in the crows'-nests fore and aft, by the deck lookouts ahead, amidships, and astern, vigilant watch was maintained. Multiply this steady eye-searching by the number of destroyers, and you may easily imagine that scarcely an inch of ocean remained for more than a minute unswept by a human eye. And yet—Fritz was there.

For two days he had lain in wait for the convoy that was now poking cautiously out through the heads; and when he attacked it was like the leap of a lone wolf on a flock, with the following rush of shepherd dogs at his throat. As he rose to take his sight at the leading steamer the *Nicholson* almost ran him down. Indeed he was going full speed astern to avoid the collision when his periscope showed above water.

It was only an instant, and the periscope was of the finger variety, an inch and a half in diameter. It was raised in that instant scarcely a foot above the water, but it was picked up by the sharp young eyes of the lookout on the *Fanning*. The submarine had submerged at once; but, rushing along his wake, the *Fanning* dropped a depth-mine that wrecked the motors, damaged the oil leads, blew off the rudder, tipped the stern up, and sent the "sub" down on a headlong dive of fully two hundred feet.

Afterward the commander said that he thought she would never stop. In a desperate effort to check her before she was crushed by deep-sea pressure, he blew out all four water-ballast tanks, and so came shooting back up with such velocity that the "sub" leaped out of the water like a breaching whale.

Instantly the *Nicholson*, which had swung on a swift circle, charged and dropped a second depth-mine as the submarine went down again. Then, as she cleared out of the way, the *Fanning* opened with her bow guns on the conning-tower, which was now showing again.

Having no rudder, the "sub" was porpoising along, now up, now down; and every time the conning-tower showed the destroyers sent a shot whistling past it. They had fired three each before the hatch flew up, and the crew came streaming out and ranged along the deck with their hands held up.

As the *Nicholson* and the *Fanning* hove alongside, covering the crew with their guns, two were seen to run back below. They were gone only a minute, but that was sufficient. Undoubtedly they had opened the sea-cocks and scuttled the vessel, for she sank three minutes later.

The crew jumped into the water, and were hauled aboard the destroyer as fast as they could catch a line, all but one who could not swim and was nearly drowned before he was seen. Then, in vivid contrast to the German practice under similar circumstances, two of our men leaped overboard and held him up until he could be hauled aboard. It was, however, too late. He died while efforts were being made to resuscitate him.

All this happened in no more than ten minutes from the dropping of the first depth-charge,—in so short a time that I was still struggling to realize that I had witnessed it,—when the executive officer hit me on the back.

"Talk about luck! Here we have been at sea for over eight months. In that time we have attacked submarines and dropped depth-charges on several. But this is the first time that I have actually seen a submarine, and here you get in on the capture. Lucky? You must be the luckiest man in the world."

How I ached to talk to those prisoners! But discipline demanded that we keep our stations; neither is a large convoy to be held up while a correspondent chatters. We moved on, leaving the *Fanning* to take the prisoners back to the base.

But I heard a good deal about them afterward. The bag consisted of one captain-lieutenant, one lieutenant, one *ober*-lieutenant, one *ober*-engineer, and thirty-six men, who could be ill spared by the *Kaiser* at this juncture in his naval affairs. As the "sub" had been out from port about six days, and had come straight to our base, it carried down with it a full complement of twelve torpedoes a loss greater than that of the submarine.

The crew appeared to be well nourished, but the faces of the officers, in particular, were deeply lined, haggard from strain and nervous anxiety. The crew appeared stolidly indifferent to capture. Indeed, after they had been given coffee and sandwiches—contrast this treatment with that accorded by a German submarine commander to the murdered crew of the *Belgian Prince*—they began to sing. When they were placed in the boats to go ashore on the first lap of their journey to a prison camp, they gave their captors three cheers.

After they were landed the *Fanning* put out again to sea, and the burial service was read over the drowned sailor before he was committed with military honours to the deep.

The prisoners were cross-examined, of course, and from a plentiful chaff of misinformation were gleaned a few kernels of wheat. The commander said, for instance, that no submarine captain who knew his business would waste a torpedo on a destroyer! That which caused our first casualty came from the hand of a "greenhorn" out on his first voyage! All very nice and friendly; but, in course of an intimate conversation with the ensign in whose cabin he was billeted for the night, he let out the fact that every U-boat keeps two torpedoes gaged for a depth of six feet—destroyers, of course!

The piece of information that most concerned us came in a radio three hours later—the base port was "closed to commerce." The harmless U-boat that would not waste a torpedo on a destroyer, not even if it went to sleep on the water, had sown the offing with mines. All those lovely evolutions of ours, swallowlike dips and swoopings, had been executed in a minefield.

I confess to a little gasp. But gasps, if you are given that way, come thick and fast on a destroyer. This interesting bit of news was quite thrown into the shade, late that afternoon, by a radio picked up in transit to the base Admiral from one of the destroyers on patrol down the coast.

U-boat just fired a torpedo at us. We have dropped a mine at head of his wake.

Evidently another "green" commander!

CHAPTER 4

The "Admiral's Busy Day"

This was the base Admiral's busy day. The next radio came from a patrol-boat that wanted to know if the captured submarine had not been engaged with them earlier in the day. It appeared that she, the patrol-boat, had plumped several shots into a submarine in the course of an artillery duel, and did not wish to be robbed of her prey. Hence a very polite inquiry as to whether the capture was due to injuries and disabilities previously inflicted.

The anxious P-boat was assured of the contrary, and, as no submarine ever travels in any other direction than the bottom with half a dozen shells in her, I have reason to believe that she got credit for a sinking.

Still the next radio told of a steamer being shelled by a submarine. She was too far away for us to help, but it drew a reminiscence from the skipper, who had joined us on the bridge.

"Someone will go to her assistance, and if she puts up a fight like the old L——, they'll stand a fine chance to be saved. We were ninety miles away when we got her first call, and while we were smoking it over the ocean just hitting the tips of the waves, the L—— kept us posted on the fight. It was like reading the rounds of a championship battle on a bulletin-board: 'Bridge shot away!' 'On fire in two places!' 'Have extinguished the fires!' 'We have thrown code books and papers overboard!'

"Since we adopted the convoy system," the skipper went on after a pause, "there is not so much of that. We have lost only one eighth of one *per cent*, of our ships, and even that small loss is principally due to hard-mouthed old skippers who will bolt the convoy if they get half a chance.

"Of course it is hard to be held down to ten knots when your boat can kick off sixteen, but it is better than going to the bottom. One chap who ran away from us on our last trip was torpedoed just ten miles ahead. The 'sub' was shelling him, too. But for the fact that our leading destroyer elevated her bow gun to the limit and by sheer luck dropped a shell within fifty feet of the 'sub' at fourteen thousand yards, he would have shared the fate of an oil-tanker whose boats we towed in last month.

"God! What a sight! After sinking the ship the 'sub' had sailed around and thrown a shell into each boat, and then machine-gunned them. Men, dead and dying, lay in the bottom of the boats. Some had been cut in two and half the body had fallen overboard. Others had arms and legs shot off. The few that survived—oh! it beggars description!

"In another case the submarine commander took away all the oars, sails, provisions, and life-belts from the boats. They even emptied the water-kegs, and went to the trouble of refilling them with sea water. Then she steamed away, leaving the unfortunate people to die of hunger and thirst two hundred miles from land. That was sheer torture—infernal deviltry that lacked even the German military excuse of extermination.

"After you have seen a few things like that you don't feel very tender toward Fritz. If we laugh when two-score poor devils are sent to the bottom the feeling springs out of righteous indignation. Fritz has drawn it on himself. He's the modern Ishmael—every man's hand against him, and his against every man. He belongs to the proscribed race."

To prove it he spoke of "Kelly," the sporting "sub" commander, who forms the single shining exception to the barbarous Hun rule. Whether "Kelly," as he signs himself, is really his name and he is a Sinn Feiner serving Germany's cause, may never be known. But one thing is certain: his point of view is truly Milesian.

"Kelly" loves his joke. Sometimes he will notify a local paper or some personage by letter that he intends to be among those present at a certain public meeting. A few days later will come a second letter criticizing all that was done and showing a remarkable knowledge of the business transacted. When he pops up alongside a fishing-boat, he pays for the fish he takes. Also he warns ships before sinking them, when possible, and gives the boats their courses to the nearest land.

On one occasion, after fighting a seven-hour duel with an American tanker that only surrendered after her ammunition ran out, "Kelly" ran alongside and congratulated the naval quartermaster in command of the gun.

"You put up a beautiful fight, sir. Sorry to have to sink you. Get into your boats, and I'll tow you to the nearest land."

He seems, in addition, to have an uncanny knowledge of the whereabouts of our destroyers, and knows all of the skippers' names.

"Pull in such and such a direction," he told one boat's crew. "In three hours you will meet the American destroyer C——. Give Captain N—— my compliments, and tell him he has a loose propeller blade. I heard it rattle when he passed over me this morning. It makes me nervous. Ask him to please have it fixed."

After an unsuccessful attack on a Canadian transport that was carrying a corps of nurses, he sent a radio after the fleeing ship: "Sorry you must go. Give my love to the nurses."

It is said that the transport replied on behalf of the nurses: "Same to you!"

From these and other tales that floated for the next hour around the bridge, I judged that "Kelly," like most personages that achieve the limelight, is gathering unto himself credit for all of those sporadic human impulses that occur in the submarine zone. Neither is the lively sailor imagination above adding a few creations of its own. "Kelly" is in danger of becoming a myth that will flourish long after the inevitable "ash-can" has been dropped on his devoted head.

But, after allowing the necessary discounts, the fact remains that such a man exists to shame by his fair fighting the methods of his brother commanders. One other thing is certain: when "Kelly" finally "gets his," a sentiment of gentle regret will pass through the fleet.

All the time we were talking, a stream of radios had been coming up to the bridge, from shore stations hundreds of miles away, from ships far out at sea, from patrol-boats and minesweepers reporting U-boats. Some were so close that we were heading across their courses. Others came from a great distance—up the Channel, the Bay of Biscay, north of Scotland, as far off as the Mediterranean.

While they were coming in, the sun rolled down its western slant and hung poised for a few moments in a glory of crimson and gold before it slipped into a purple sea. Above stretched a dappled vault that blazed in rainbow colour, save where in the west a great tear in the radiant tapestries revealed a wall of pale jade.

It was intensely beautiful, so lovely that the mind refused further commerce with the petty squabbles of man; refused to picture the sea

U. S. BATTLESHIP GOING AT FULL SPEED

DECK SCENE ON U. S. S. *TEXAS*, SHOWING HER MAIN BATTERIES

murderers who were lying in wait beneath those jewelled waters. But they were there. Out of that cloud glory, over the sleepy, beautiful sea, came a strange radio.

"Listen to the chattering of the little 'subs.'" The skipper chuckled as he read it:

> Have you seen any ships today? Look out for the strafed American destroyers. Muller does not answer my call; I am afraid they have sunk him.

A little later came a second call for help—again too far for our service. Other radios that floated in late that night told how a derelict, deserted by captain and crew, had been towed in by a patrol and safely beached.

Of those streaming radios never a one that did not produce a tale or reminiscence from the "bridge." Usually tragic, recording the deaths of fine ships and brave men, their grimness was shot through here and there with a gleaming thread of humour.

Such was the case of the *M—— L——* , a fine munitions ship that was carrying a million-dollar cargo when she was torpedoed a hundred miles from the base. From afar the Admiral sent an anxious inquiry concerning her condition and progress. He received in reply:

> We are making three and a half knots, but it is a d—— long way to Tipperary.

It was, alas! The poor ship foundered at sea.

Then there was the *Lovely Lucy*, a trim little steamer that strayed away from her convoy in a thick mist. Late that evening a radio came in from a destroyer that had just picked up the estray:

> What did you do to the *Lovely Lucy?* Found her at dusk, without an escort, zigzagging wildly through the mist.

Also there were tales of Homeric encounters between English and German "subs." Fancy a head-on collision under water! Well, it occurred. Two came together one evening at dusk, backed off, fired a torpedo apiece, then lost each other in the darkness.

Another English "sub" popped out of the water one day alongside a steamer that was being sunk by a Fritzer's shell-fire. The steamer lay between him and the Fritzer; so, diving, the Englishman waited till Fritz came sailing around, then put a torpedo into his solar plexus. For some reason—perhaps it was loot from the steamer—Fritz had some cases of beer piled on his deck. His end is crudely but vividly described in the report of the English commander:

> When he went up, the air was full of beer, blood, Boches, and broken bottles.

That evening displayed destroyer life at its best. A brilliant moon—which the "bridge" most fluently cursed for an ally of the Boche—laid a path of silver along the sleepy sea. Our boat laid her long, slim cheek against the slow, soft waves as lovingly as a girl on that of her lover. From the deck below the mixed tinkle of a mandolin and guitar came floating up to the bridge, accompanying a mixed repertoire of ragtime and those sentimental ballads which the sailor so dearly loves.

It had quite the flavour of a Coney Island picnic; but, every hour, a dark figure slowly raised and lowered the guns and swung them the round of the firing circle. The gunners were taking no chances of the mechanism "freezing" through cold stiffened grease, or of failure of the electric sighting lamps.

CHAPTER 5

Winter Work

This remarkable weather held till we dropped our convoy well out of the danger zone and picked up a second inward bound at a rendezvous a hundred miles farther south. Two days later we gave half of our charge to a British flotilla, which led it on other ways. We had expected to drop the remaining ships on the following morning; but destiny, alias the base Admiral, decreed otherwise. Piqued, no doubt, by his small bag of one small ship the preceding week, Fritz had broken into waters that, for him, were extremely unsafe, and was shooting right and left, like a drunken cowboy on the Fourth of July. A radio informed us at dawn:

Area X is closed.

This meant the delivery of each ship at its individual port. During the additional day and night required to do this "subs" were operating to the right of us, "subs" to the left of us, "subs" in front, "subs" behind us. Often we crossed their courses; but, though they sank several ships that were unconvoyed, they left us strictly alone.

Already the "blimps," sausage balloons, patrol-boats, hydroplanes, and destroyers were going after them like swarming hornets. The piratical nest was soon exterminated and the sea opened again. But we had not escaped without alarm. Twice "general quarters" sounded and we all piled out—a certain correspondent with his hair standing on end—to find that the alarm was caused by a short circuit. Twice in the night porpoises charged the ship along gleaming wakes of phosphorescence, and turned the hair of the engine-room crews gray with emergency calls for full speed astern. But without hitch or mishap we delivered our ships at their destinations.

All the last day the wind had been stiffening. After we headed back for the base it raised to half a gale, real destroyer weather. As we sat at supper in the ward-room that night, the twinkle in Admiral Sims's eye was recalled when, with celerity that almost equalled a sleight-of-hand, the table-cloth slid with its load of food and dishes swiftly to the floor.

The casual manner in which the steward accepted and swept up the ruin betrayed familiarity with the phenomenon. When he reset the table we held the tablecloth down, and had got safely to the coffee when, with his cup poised at his lip, the skipper tobogganed on his chair—back to the transom. Swallowing the coffee while she hung in the balance, he came back to us on the return roll.

Profiting by his commander's example, the executive officer, who sat opposite, had hooked his ankles around those of the table; so he took it with him to the other transom. When it returned, further journeyings were restrained by a rope lashing; but that, unfortunately, had no effect on the motion. It kept on just the same; grew worse and more of it.

By midnight the vessel was rearing like a frightened horse and rolling like a barrel churn, a queer mixture of metaphor and motion. She would rear, shiver with rage, as if she were trying to shake the bridge off her back, then plunge forward in a wild buck with her back humped and screws in the air.

It was sickening. When she did her best and beastliest, the waves would drop from under, leaving two thirds of her length exposed; then, when the thousand tons of her came down on the water, she raised everything animate and inanimate that was not bolted down to the deck. I was lifted so often out of my bunk that I spent almost half the night in midair, and am now quite convinced of the possibility of levitation. By morning my sides were bruised from striking the sides of the bunk; my skin was sore from constant shaking.

I confess to making a modest breakfast on one dill pickle. While I was engaged in the gingerly consumption thereof the ward-room comforted me with the news that this was "only half a blow," and that we might expect the other half before we made port. They assured me it was fair weather by comparison with a nine days' gale they had ridden out last month; fine weather measured by a blow the preceding trip, when for thirty-six hours the waves swept her from stem to stern, the living compartments were flooded, everything and everybody was wet, freezing to boot, while the wind howled through the rigging at a hundred and ten miles an hour. Think of it, you folks who live in warm houses and work in steam-heated offices.

Fair or fine, the bridge was nearly dipping its ends when I climbed up there after—after the dill pickle. At every plunge her nose would go under a solid sea, and we would have to duck to avoid flying water that went over the top of the bridge. Watery mist veiled the tossing seas. All night we had been shoved along by a five-knot current running by dead reckoning. It was now impossible to take a "sight" to establish position; so, just as a lost boy might inquire his way from a policeman, we ran inshore to a lightship to get our position.

The lightship-keeper megaphoned a direction which in unnautical language amounted to this: If we would proceed so many blocks to the northward, then take the first turning to the left after we passed a lighthouse, we should come into a harbour where lay the half dozen ships we were to escort back to our base.

The direction proved correct. As the convoy came filing out after us a few hours later, I was able to see for myself one of those humorous flashes that sometimes lighten the gloom of the radios. Perceiving still another vessel in harbour after the convoy came out, our skipper sent a radio to inquire whether she would care to make use of our escort.

He received a polite reply:

Thanks very much. Think I'll stay in. I was torpedoed going out yesterday.

The delivery of this convoy at the base the following day completed my cruise. In a period of twelve days we had steamed sixteen hundred miles and convoyed a total number of sixty vessels in and out of port.

As I sit in cosy London chambers, writing before a cheery sea-coal fire, and think of my late messmates out upon those dangerous waters, the thing that stands out most clearly in my remembrance is their loyalty to one another, the friendly spirit of the fine, clean sailor lads, the mutual respect for each other of officers and crews, the unswerving belief of both in their ships and commanders; finally, the faith and complete devotion of every man in the fleet to Sims, their Admiral.

I shall not soon forget my last view of the fleet. Looking down from a high hill behind the town, I could see the destroyers that had cruised with us lying like tired dogs on the harbour's bosom. Far out on the heads signal lights began to wink and blink, no doubt the tale of a submarine. From the heights to my left the Admiralty station answered. Then, very slowly, a destroyer opened one eye and blinked a response. Shortly thereafter three slim, dark shapes slid downstream and headed out to sea.

I was for home, but Sims's captains were again on the job.

The "circus is continuous."

CHAPTER 6

Shore Leave—the Other Side
of Destroyer Life

"You must go and see the Men's Naval Club," said my friend the
ensign. "It is the finest show in all this circus."

It was he that had christened the American flotilla "Sims's Circus,"
because of the dazzle paint, which shamed by its rainbow daubing the
ring-streaked zebras of Barnum and Bailey's famous aggregation. He
had already initiated me into the Yacht Club, where that minor portion of a ship's company known as the "bridge" rests from the sea and
warms its chilled legs at a sea-coal fire. Also we had run upriver in a
motor-boat to a golf links where nerves over-strained by incessant
watching for torpedoes, that come as swift death in the night, may be
relaxed; whereafter I had been introduced to one of the "firesides" the
country gentry place at the service of weather-worn officers. Green
grass and a fireside—these are the things a sailor always craves.

Speaking of grass, I had "hiked" six miles that morning with five
skippers, who prowled through the fields like cats delicately feeling
the velvet turf with their feet. Also I had voyaged with them through
mined seas, chasing the elusive submarine; so the Men's Naval Club
alone remained to complete the picture of destroyer life in the danger
zone.

★★★★★★

Dusk was falling thickly over the harbour when we walked down
to the quay-walls. Here, under the shelter of a high hill, the tides
lapped softly around the hundred-odd vessels whose golden lights
dotted the gloomy waters with shimmering reflections. But, having
come in from the sea only that morning, I knew that beyond the harbour heads the swells were running mountains high under the urge of

33

a heavy wind. Out there a score of our destroyers were now heaving their noses up to the dark skies, again plunging head downward into a watery abyss. But we had finished our trick, at that. With a reminiscent but comfortable shudder, we turned to watch the boats whose red and green lights moved like swift moths between the ships and the quay.

Under the golden glare of the stair lights, the dark mass of a boat would take form and resolve into a crowd of figures topped by two-score of bright, upturned faces. Clear cut, simple and direct in speech, quiet and courteous in manner, they looked all that I know them to be—the finest type of the world's young manhood. As boat after boat unloaded, there came a toy whistle, and the lights of a train came around a curve into the station at the end of the quay.

"The 'Doves' Special," the ensign explained. "Having more money to spend, our boys cut the Irish lads up in the city out of their girls, and so many ructions resulted that we had to put it out of bounds. But when the mountain wouldn't come to Mahomet, he just naturally went to the mountain. As the sailors can't go to the girls, the girls come to the sailors. Hundreds of them come down every night on this train."

The "doves" were already pairing when we gained back to the street. The sidewalks rang to the tippity-tap of small feet moving in rhythm with rolling sailor treads. Under the electric glare of a shop window, the face of a pretty colleen flashed out, the cheeks fresh and high-coloured from persistent kissing by climatic fogs and rains, the Irish blue eyes and red mouth laughing up at a tall sailor lad. Her speech ran over her white teeth in a torrent too swift for his ears. His apology, delivered in a delightfully soft Southern drawl, drifted back to us:

"Ah really doan' know what's the mattah with me. Ah 'm that dull I doan' seem to heah ya.' Will you-all please to say that ovah ag'n?"

The repetition was evidently quite satisfactory. His hand tightened on her arm. The arm pulled the hand close to her side in a little squeeze. Then they passed into the gloom beyond the window lights. It was all very pretty and innocent—as young love always is. Already this nightly pairing has resulted in a few international marriages of the natural healthy kind that cannot be held up as awful warning in the Sunday supplements.

Following in this couple's wake, we come presently to the one native Irish attempt to supply the flotilla with amusement. If five thousand English or French sailors were to be suddenly "based" in some small American city, it goes without saying that a week would see it transformed by enterprising amusement caterers into a miniature Coney Island. But a roller-skating floor laid down in a ramshackle barn on top of a hill was all that the need had here produced.

Its quality may be judged by the fact that, just after we stepped in, a burly destroyer fire-man and his little colleen partner shot through the end wall and down the hill with ease and celerity that surpassed the famous "Flivver Four" in its best movie stunt. Fortunately, they were not hurt. The shriek of horror that followed the crash had scarcely subsided before the fireman lifted the girl back up through the breach. Quite unconcerned, they joined again in the skating.

Music there was none; none of the moonlight numbers or kaleidoscopic light changes beloved of skating fans in American rinks. Neither is a skating sailor the most graceful of nature's creatures. As the lads struck out, right and left, their wide trousers moved with raven flappings in rhythm with the graceful swing of their partners' skirts. The arm movement of beginners was also wonderful to behold; for, when uncertain of his balance, a sailor reaches naturally for a rope. Such snatchings at each other and the empty air! But what cared they for appearances? The night was young, the floor good, their partners pretty. What more could be asked of the Fates by Youth? Mingled with laughter and small screams, the roar and scrape of their skates followed us downhill to the Naval Club.

A low, rambling building, the club squats on the quay-wall, so close to the water that one might pitch a stone on to the destroyers whose crews meet the cheer of its lighted windows coming into port on dark nights. Through its hospitable doorway we passed at once into a wide, clean kitchen and dining-room, where bright lights, white tables, and appetizing odours combined in the best of welcomes.

Half a hundred of the lads we had seen come ashore were turning their appetites loose on short orders of steak, chops, fried chicken, and the like, served with vegetables, bread, butter, and mighty mugs of hot "Java"; all at prices no higher than those that obtained in the United States before the war. Nothing would suit the boatswain in charge but that I should test the fare; and, having eaten with the fo'castle messes during my cruise,—having seen, moreover, the captain call for the men's dinner in preference to his own,—I am in position to say that in the American Navy the man before the mast eats as well, if not better, than his officer.

Like other men, however, sailors do not live by bread alone, and the Club supplies other needs—a library, reading, writing and billiard rooms, dormitories, baths; most important of all from the men's point of view, a cinema show. The pictures shown are of both British and American manufacture, but the men naturally prefer the home-made article. When a "Fairbanks" or "Pickford" number is shown—well, the theatre, which seats at least eight hundred, is packed with officers and men. And how they enjoy them! Unless you have been bucking the big seas for a few months in a jack-knife of a destroyer, with mines and torpedoes loose all around, you are not in position to feel the unalloyed bliss to be obtained from the sight of "Dug" Fairbanks perched on a chandelier while a saloon brawl seethes beneath.

Neither can you feel, as these lads felt, sympathy for the simple girl who endures the horrors of virtuous poverty—on the screen for the modest compensation of five thousand dollars a week. When, after the customary harassments, she snuggles into the manly hero's arms, safe at last from further persecutions, a sigh always passes through the sailor audience. You know—that is, if you were ever young you know—that the embrace has recalled to each a whiff of rice powder, the caressing touch of a soft cheek, the thrill of clinging lips, the wonderful evening when his first girl yielded her young body to his arms.

To see the club at its best, however, you must go there, as I did, to a Saturday evening concert. The savoury odours that greeted me at the door were, if possible, richer and more enticing. Certain tootles and trumpetings mingled with them, filtering in from the theatre, where the flotilla bandmaster—a pay clerk who bears up bravely under the handicap of having two thirds of his orchestra always afloat—was drilling the residue left him by this cruel war. There have been occasions when its vicissitudes left only the drum and trombones, but tonight he was rejoicing in a fair instrumental balance.

It is a point with all of the destroyer skippers to make port on this night, if they can. Indeed, if a tithe of the curses that have been wished on laggard six-knot convoys ever came home to roost, the U-boat would win hands down in the underseas war. By eight o'clock one could see through a thick tobacco haze that the pit and gallery were crowded with officers and men. Thick! It was so thick that the calcium beam for the first picture stabbed through like a sunbeam into a dusty room. By the time the orchestra split the evening wide open with a rattling march, the old familiar HO^2 was conspicuous by its absence. How the trombones secured atmosphere enough for their purposes, I really do not know. But they did: the noise was there to prove it.

After the overture, the flotilla comedian, who had once done "time" on a vaudeville circuit, gave a sympathetic account of how "it takes a long, tall, brown-skinned gal to make a cull'rd preacher lay his Bible down." He was really very good—so good that, though the lads smacked their lips and said "Oooooh-ooh!" at the pretty model in *The Artist and the Ice-man*, this was merely the persiflage of the budding male animal: it did not diminish the comedian's laurels.

It requires, however, a sentimental ballad of the good old-fashioned sort to get really under a sailor's skin; and this happened when a raw old sea-dog, who looked as if music and all its affinities were quite alien to his soul, produced a fine tenor voice from his capacious chest, and rendered therewith a touching ditty about tears and fears and smiles and wiles, sighs, blue eyes, and similar of love's phenomena. Talk about a hit! Not till he had sung all he knew about mother, home, sweethearts, wives, not till he had wrung their deepest and tenderest feelings dry, did they let that man off the stage.

Sentimental, you say? Bosh! What do we landsmen know of sentiment! Surrounded by love, with a surfeit of femininity always under our eyes, we are not in position to know the real thing. That which would be sentimentality in a landsman is genuine feeling in a sailor, honest and sincere, raised to the nth degree by long dreaming in the cold night watches on dangerous seas. Living on the borderland between life and death, expectant always of the torpedo or mine that will send him across, love, friendship, and affection, the finest of human relations, are in the destroyer sailor deepened and intensified.

I quite understand the lad who said, with deep conviction: "All women are pretty." He merely reflected truth as mirrored in the sailor soul. And many a landsman's wife will envy the girl whose destroyer husband writes to her every day. His letters, it is true, arrive in batches of fifteen and twenty; but, happy in her knowledge of the deep love in which his pen is dipped, she reads them over and over again.

Asked by a comrade what in the world he could find to write about in the narrow life at sea, one husband answered with cryptic truth:

"My lad, there's a whole lot of things hidden yet from you."

This husband was more fortunate than another poor fellow, into whose envelope, addressed to his wife, the naval censor slipped by mistake the ardent love-letter of another man. The writing was different, of course, but the signature, "Your loving Bill," was the same. With deep feminine craft, she argued that it would be quite easy for him to get some other man to pen the epistle, and it is said that a combined affidavit of the captain, censor, and crew to the effect that her "Bill" was almost ridiculously true was required to persuade her to give him another trial. It also goes without saying—every husband knows it—that, let "Bill" walk never so straitly, he will be under suspicion for the rest of his life.

The same deep sailor feeling turned up again when, after the concert, the boatswain showed me the portraits of his young wife and two babies, while serving a stirrup-cup of Java in his room. They hung over his cot, where his eyes opened upon them in the morning. I wish she could have seen him look at them! But she must know.

From them his glance went to a framed portrait of Admiral Sims that stood leaning against the wall, and, while sipping the Java, we judiciously debated as to the best place to hang it in the Club. If the good man had had his own wish, the Admiral would undoubtedly have gone up between his children and his wife. But that would not have been fair to the other men. It must be hung in a good light, where everyone could see it the moment they stepped into the club. Just where it was eventually placed I cannot say. But this much I do know: judging from the keen disappointment of the entire flotilla when illness prevented the Admiral from being with them at the club last Christmas Eve, it does not matter much. His image stands next to that of the home folks in the imagination of his men.

Going home, I paused to watch the busy boats, with their brilliant moth lights, ferrying a thousand sailors back to their floating homes. The roar of the rink had died on the hill. With the exception of a few residents, the little doves had flown back to their cotes on the ten-thirty express.

At the quay stairs the sputtering arc lights glared down on a dense blue mass that was spotted here and there with the white service caps of the patrols. It were dangerous business to have tried to embark as many civilians from that one stair. But, as each boat called her ship's name and pulled in, she instantly filled from a stream of leaping cat-like figures; in half a minute shoved off again. Even the few "wildies" under care of the patrols, who had worshiped with Bacchus instead of the naval Muses, dropped in like babes to their cradles. By eleven they were all gone. Out on the harbour the golden reflections died as ship after ship doused her lights.

It seemed so happy and peaceful; yet, out there beyond the heads, the black seas were still running mountainously. Down in their troughs, climbing their watery peaks a score of destroyers were moving with their convoys on their appointed ways. Already those dark, tempestuous seas had snatched away a score of our lads. Within a week they were to engulf a destroyer with half her crew. Some of those I had just seen off would never come back again; their warm dreamings in the night watches, glowing feeling, would be quenched by the cold waves. But—the others would "carry on": go out with a smile to face the ever-present death, return for another brief holiday at next week's end.

Chapter 7

"When Greek Meets Greek"

"There it is!" exclaimed the Commander.

"It" was a periscope.

Time was required for my landsman's eyes to pick the foot or two of slender, swaying red out of the green seas some six hundred yards away. Fortunately, it did not belong to a Hun, for the forward and aft periscopes were exactly in line. Our compatriot—with whom we were playing the war game—had us dead to rights for the torpedo that, half a minute later, whizzed across our stern.

"It would have hit a U-boat," the Commander passed favourable comment. "They range much longer than ours. Our turn. Take your last look at the sun and scenery, for you won't see them again for a week."

You see, I was going out with him on an eight-day patrol. The green farms, dotted with white cottages, that ran steeply down the slopes of a frowning mountain to the jade-green Irish sea, were really very beautiful. But this submarine business was far too novel and interesting to waste time on scenery. I followed at once down the funnel hatchway to the interior depths below.

My previous conceptions of a submarine had been entirely formed by those coloured magazine illustrations wherein huge brown cigars float in a greenish haze with fishes and seaweed posed in the foreground. A donkey-engine inside about completed the idea which was now quite shocked out of existence by the formidable array of clocks and gages, levers, wheels, switch-boards, telephones, and speaking-tubes that caused the central operating chamber to look like the crazed nightmare of a mad inventor.

Gazing thereon, I felt a vast respect for the commander, a man who knew not only what it was all about, but who could take the whole works apart, if necessary, and put them together again without acquiring the traditional bucketful of extra parts. The half dozen men who stood or sat in front of the said clocks and gages looked equally resourceful. They moved like clockwork themselves under a sudden stream of orders:

"Flood forward tank!"

A petty officer read off the gage in hundreds of gallons till the order came: "Secure!"

So, likewise, with the centre and after tanks. Whereafter smaller "trimming tanks" were "flooded" or "blown" till the boat floated in perfect equilibrium at the depth required.

All this had been absorbed through my ears and one eye—the other being glued to the periscope. It was queer to watch the pointed deck sink slowly under the green swells, which then mounted the conning-tower, leaving exposed to view only the other periscope. All things—green water, farms, white cottages, dark frowning Irish mountain—showed crystal clear to my gaze; for a periscope lens is about one power telescopic.

Friend Enemy had now emerged, and was steaming along the surface, doing his best to look like a Hun. But, just as I swung the periscope round to watch him, a green wave slapped the lens in the eye. Instinctively I wiped my own optic, and when I looked again—it was into an aquarium filled with the aforesaid green haze and frothing bubbles.

My other eye showed the commander and his men working the boat on a course that would intercept Friend Enemy at easy distance for slaughter. A torpedoing had always appeared to me as quite a simple business. You just lay in wait like a thug at a street corner till a Hun happened along, then shot a "fish" into his belly. Now I learned something of the tide rips, currents, reefs and shoals that may bring your benevolent intention to naught.

After we poked up our periscope again and sighted our quarry dead ahead, we still had to round a rock that obstinately refused to get out of the way. The commander's comments upon it could never be printed on this page. They gave a picturesque flavour to streaming orders that were suddenly capped by his shout:

"Fire!"

Followed a grating and sizzling as the torpedo leaped from the tube. It covered two hundred yards before I picked up the white wake shooting as fast as an express train at Friend Enemy. Half a minute later—alas, that he had not been a Hun!—its soft practice head crumpled against his steel sides.

"Now—if we can do as well on a Fritz !" The commander modestly hid a natural exultation. "Let's go.'

And go we did, proceeding at leisurely speed toward our patrol across the U-boat routes. It was going to be a hard siege—eight days cooped up, without sight of the sun.

The commander had laughed at the idea of my going: said I should be bored to death; probably die of seasickness complicated by *ennui*. But, with a grim determination to put off the evil moment as long as possible, I started on a tour of the boat, beginning in the bows at the torpedo-room, where two men sat reading old magazines in front of the hydrophones. Donning the ear-pieces of their apparatus, I heard at once, with great distinctness, the swirl and wash of our twin screws.

The beat of a propeller can, indeed, be heard for miles, and only the week before one of our "subs" had followed up a U-boat, intending to ram it under water. *To ram it*, I repeat.

What a situation readymade for a fiction writer! Equal to the best of Jules Verne. To a "blimp" or seaplane, had one happened to be hovering above that morning, their manoeuvring would have presented a remarkable spectacle—the U-boat, a purple shadow, lazily swimming through the pale green vaults of the sea; the American, a dark steel shark, in swift pursuit; also, unseen by the latter, a second U-boat stealthily hunting the hunter.

Surely a remarkable situation; and the cleverest stage-manager could not have invented a more astonishing climax. The thing that happened outmovied the movies. Close and closer the American drew to his quarry. Closer and closer drew the second Hun astern. At last, poking up his periscope, the former saw the periscope of his prey sticking up out of the water dead ahead. He was just getting ready to charge and stick his sharp steel prow into the other's metal vitals, when—something happened. *Boom!* a huge green geyser "that looked like a water-spout" rose under the Hun's bows.

What was it? One of two things—either the first Hun fired a torpedo that exploded prematurely on leaving the tube, or he was hit by a torpedo fired at the American by his brother Hun. The effect was the same—to wit, he sank immediately, and for further details concerning his finish we are indebted to the hydrophones on the American boat, which mapped out his death flounderings while he flew round and round like a poisoned fish.

Undoubtedly he was trying to come up. But, whether he exhausted his batteries—which happens quickly at high speed submerged—or descended on a shallow spiral to depths where he was crushed, we shall never know. Sufficient that a sudden deadly silence ensued, in which could be clearly heard the signals of his companion, calling like an old ewe for her lost lamb. Warned by these of the new enemy, the American turned with the intention of carrying out on him the same benevolent intention he nursed for his companion. But, taking warning by the fate of his brother, Hun Number Two turned and headed away at high speed—presumably for Heligoland.

This remarkable history—as told to me by the commander of the American boat and his executive officer—closed with a touch of that grim humour which so often shows like a seam of gold in these tragedies of the underseas. For, in violation of that commandment which forbids the coveting of one's neighbour's goods and chattels, both officers had set their hearts on acquiring the Hun's periscope.

"Ten foot in the clear?" the commander regretfully remarked. "Wouldn't need to show your conning-tower, even in rough weather, with *that* periscope."

"With a four-power lens," his executive lamented. "Just like the one I looked through when the *Deutschland* lay at Newport. Lordy, I should like to have taken it away from him. It was sacrilege to sink it."

Returning to the torpedo-chamber from this wide digression—with its rows of extra torpedoes, shining steel "fish," as the sailors call them, also the complex array of clocks, wheels, and levers around the steel doors of the tubes, it is easily the most interesting place on board. About it hangs the atmosphere of war, for it is the fighting end of the ship—its reason for existence. Apart from its war uses, it also affords sleeping quarters for a dozen men in pipe-bracket hammocks at the other end.

In the next chamber eight other men slept with three officers, one corner being fenced off for the commander, by a high-backed desk into a tiny ward-room three feet wide by six in length. Two other officers were stowed like bales of cloth on shelves two feet wide and eighteen inches high. The wireless room, three feet by four, was crammed under the second officer's bunk, with head-room of less than five feet. A cot had been set up in the narrow aisle for me—from which I may say, in passing, that I was ejected every night by the rolling of the boat in surface cruising: said excursion usually being made in company with seven clattering pails, a host of sea-boots, and the drawers of the commander's desk whenever he forgot to lock them. Also certain hectic dreams of pursuing U-boats were given verisimilitude by the wrigglings of a sailor taking "gravity tests "of the acid batteries under my bed at unholy hours of the night.

Next came the central operating chamber already described; then the galley and mess-room, shared alike by officers and men. Down its centre ran a swing table. An electric stove and cupboards for food stores filled one side of the chamber, the other being occupied by an overflow meeting of switchboards, levers, gages, and wheels from the operating chamber. Still next came the engine-room, shared by powerful Diesel engines for surface cruising, with electrical machinery for underseas work. Lastly, the "shaft alley," which is also a machine-shop fitted with lathes and other tools. Such concentration I have never seen. Yet, cramped as the living quarters seemed to me, they are commodious by comparison with the English boats, *roomy* by contrast with the French.

The close companionship forced on officers and men by these narrow quarters naturally does not make for the formal discipline maintained on a battleship. But what is lost in form is more than made up in substance—the material substance implied by that thorough knowledge of one another which is invaluable in a ship's company where the lives of all depend on any one. Nowhere in the world is a man so quickly known by his works as on a submarine. As the commander put it:

You cannot do any four-flushing on these boats. Your crew soon finds you out—and you them.

By the time I had finished my tour the crew had settled down to the regular routine of subseas life. Half were in bed; the others scattered through the chambers on various watches. Six men and an officer closely watched the clocks and gages in the operating-chamber which record the depth, speed, and pressure; for eternal vigilance is the price of safety. A submarine differs not a whit from a soaked plank. A shove will send it straight to the bottom. Or it is like a feather floating in the air, at the mercy of every downward current. And, once let it start down, it is difficult to stop it short of depths where a boat is crushed like an egg-shell by deep-sea pressure.

So delicate was our equilibrium, it was seriously disturbed when, that evening, the men moved from their bunks forward back to the galley for supper. The transfer of their weight could be offset by "blowing" its equivalent out of the after tanks while "flooding "the same amount of water forward; but after a commander has once obtained his "trim" he does not like to change it. A temporary balance was achieved by driving the boat at greater speed. While the men were eating, the commander illustrated all this with the story of a bit of carelessness that almost cost the lives of the entire crew.

A wrong manifold was opened, and flooded fifteen thousand gallons of water into the forward tank. Instantly she dived so quickly that the hands of the depth-gages there seemed to spin around. In deep water we should have been done in at once. As it was, we brought up and stuck, nose down, in the bottom mud three hundred feet below. That meant a pressure of one hundred and eighty pounds to the square foot on every inch of our surface. You will realize what that means when I say that the hatch-cover up there, while little more than eighteen inches in diameter, was sustaining a pressure of two hundred and forty thousand pounds.

We could not blow the extra water out of the tanks, for the pressure outside was greater than that of our compressed air within. It really looked as though we were there for keeps; yet the men behaved beautifully, calm, cool, not a bit excited. When I awakened the sleepers and ordered them all into the shaft alley astern, they went back there yawning and stretching like sleepy kids. I tell you, even in that moment of stress I was proud of them.

That, you see, was our only chance—to put all the extra weight we could astern and try and break her down. Thirty husky sailors at the extreme end of a hundred-and-sixty foot boat exercises as much leverage as a swarm of bees at the end of a single stalk of wheat. They broke her down, all right—pried her nose out of the mud. We still could not blow the tanks; but we had our power, and went full speed ahead. She rose under the pull of the rudder to levels where we could blow, and after that she shot up like a rocket and fell back with a flop in the water.

He concluded with a pause that was far more impressive than the most dramatic utterance:

I tell you, the sun looked good to all of us.

And why wouldn't it! Of all possible deaths, to be sealed in a steel tomb at the bottom of the sea is the least inviting. Sea and sky also looked good to me when, at ten-thirty that evening, we emerged and opened up the hatch. Though so late, the long northern twilight still shed a chastened light over the sea. Westward, a curtain of crimson and gold, split by long horizontal tears of pale jade and black velvet, overhung a purple sea. Far off an Irish mountain raised its dim dark head—too far away to be of any use to us if Fritz happened to see us first.

Nothing forces on man a sense of his own in-significance so powerfully as the infinite loneliness of the sea. The conning-tower upheld us, small specks of life in the midst of that great gray spread of waters, human atoms at loose in a universe they never can know or understand.

I could not help thinking of that Allied submarine which sailed from our port, never to return. Day after day, the commander's wife still goes down to the pier-head, looking for his return—a subject of pity for the sympathetic Irish peasants. And I thought too of that fine officer of ours, a guest on board, whose wife at home nurses just as fondly the hope that he will come back some day from a German prison to her and the babe he has never seen.

Than this there can be no greater tragedy—to nurse *the hope that maketh the heart sick*. Death, at least, is final, allowing the spirits to make such readjustments to life as it may. The cold waves that lapped the foot of the conning-tower brought that tragedy very close—made it as vividly real as though I had seen it with my own eyes. Also they stimulated the imagination. The feeling that Fritz was out there training a torpedo on us grew as the twilight faded. It had attained its full strength when the lookout suddenly spoke:

"Looks like a torpedo to starboard, sir!"

The second officer, who had the watch, took one sharp look. "Porpoise—I *hope?*"

Though there was no time even to change course, they had spoken as quietly as though that white streak leaping at us out of the dusk were not a matter for heart disease. It was all over in ten seconds, but I know one person who did not breathe until, with a *whoof*, the streak passed beneath us. Porpoise it was.

Silence reigned in the boat when I returned below—for matter of that, it reigned there most of the time. The composite impression left by my eight days below sea is of silence and darkness and dampness that filled; the sleeping-chambers day and night, for it is unethical to turn on a light. Shaving, if one must do it, is performed by the low glow of a half-candle-power bulb. While lying in bed—which was most of the time, the soggy atmosphere makes so strongly for sleep I was never more than half conscious of dark shapes forming and fading in the gloom at the changing of the watch, for sailors move more softly than cats. I was roused oftener and more completely by sudden elevations of my heels over my head by changes in the "trim," or by the rolling when we went up to the surface at night. Then fresh, sweet air would be forced through the boat to clean out the odours and foulness collected during the day.

At any time the men do not talk much. They just sit at their posts, reading or thinking—no doubt of their mothers, sisters, and sweethearts at home. In eating, watching, and sleeping the days and nights passed, one as much like the other as two peas in the same pod. If sociability appeared at all, it was during the few golden moments allowed for the smoking of two cigarettes per man per day back in the engine-room.

Though cork-lined, the boat began to sweat on the third day out from the condensation of the warmer inner air by the cold sea without. Clothing became first damp, then moist, finally wet. My shoes were soaked by the streaming moisture on the floor. Such submarines carry only two gallons of water a day for each man for all purposes; two pints is considered about the correct amount for ablutions. This is mentioned not in a spirit of criticism. My own batting average at the basin was below normal—I think about one pint. It merely emphasizes the fact that nine and twenty greasy humans contribute the characteristic flavours of our race to an atmosphere already surcharged with bilge, fuel oil, fried sausage, boiling cabbage, aided and abetted by a touch of chlorine gas from the batteries, all reinforced in turn by the good old CO^2, *alias* carbon dioxid, which is always with us.

Not that manful attempts are not made to purify the atmosphere. All the livelong day it is drawn through a circulation system which extracts the CO^2. This does not, however, re-store the used oxygen, which is so depleted that after twelve hours a struck match will not burn. A cigarette that I succeeded in lighting, one evening, at the flares of three matches, went out, though I puffed never so strongly. However, it causes no serious inconvenience. After seventeen hours submerged I breathed a little more quickly; my pulse was slightly accelerated; I felt a trifle feverish, and panted a little moving about. But in none of this was there cause for alarm. Pure oxygen is carried in flasks for emergencies; but, as long as the atmosphere retains fifteen *per cent.*, it is not renewed. The British have worked as low as twelve *per cent.*, and have even run it down to ten, in experiments, without serious effects. So, while not exactly what one might call salubrious, the atmosphere of our "subs" may be considered relatively healthful.

The monotony of this odorous existence of ours was broken, one day, by the dull, rending reports of distant depth-mines; whereby I was introduced to a new danger that had not figured, so far, in my tables of probable life in a submarine. For your Allied "sub" is somewhat of an Ishmaelite, with everybody's hand against it. An "oil slick" on the surface, you see, is an "oil slick," to be treated as such—with depth-mines—by every destroyer that comes along. If it happens to proceed from the bilge you have just pumped out—well, in the words of the machinist's mate with whom I discussed the matter in the engine-room, "You are simply out of luck." Your hydrophones, of course, can give you warning of a destroyer's approach; whereafter it is up to you to emerge and make signals. Far more dangerous are the "blimps" and seaplanes that swoop soundlessly upon you from the heavens.

The machinist's mate described one such encounter:

We were moseying along about our lawful business when—*boom!* out goes all of our lights! We couldn't hear a thing, so up we goes to take a look. And what d'you think the first officer spies when he peeks through the periscope? A darned big blimp circling for another shot.

'Now what d' you make of that?' he calls to the skipper, who'd jumped to the other periscope.

'What do I make of it!' he yells back. 'Blow your tanks, quick! That's what I make of it.'

And we weren't a bit too soon; for, as the skipper threw up the hatch, back come the blimp at seventy miles an hour. 'Just in time, old top!' her commander yells down through his megaphone. 'I'd have got you next shot!'

One time, too, a destroyer took three cracks at us. It was easy shooting, nice range, and he oughtn't to have missed. So, as soon as the skipper could get his wigwag going he signalled back, just like it was bad target practice: 'One high and two wide.' He didn't add that the 'high' just grazed the conning-tower.

The commander, who came back just then to the engine-room for his daily smoke, added another experience:

> We had heard screws, and, coming up to investigate, we found ourselves in the dead centre of an American convoy with our largest transport on the beam. It was a cinch the periscope had been seen, so there was nothing to do but emerge. And talk about a sensation! A naked madman breaking into a young ladies' seminary could not have raised half the fuss. About fourteen destroyers charged us from all around, with guns trained and depth-mines poised, and every naval gunner in the convoy was yelling for a chance. Of course we went to shooting signals, and when they realized that we belonged to them, you never in all your life saw such a disappointed lot. They circled around and bawled us out through their megaphones in the sixteen possible ways. I found out a whole lot I hadn't known about myself in a few short minutes. When I asked what I should do—stay there or dive?—they told me just where I could go to in just three words. I was darned glad when they passed on— grouchy lot!

About as dangerous to Allied "subs" are those enthusiastic skippers of the mercantile marine who are determined to "get them a U-boat" while the getting is still good. After the skipper had gone forward, the machinist's mate produced another crucial instance from his varied experience:

> We'd heard this bird's screw, and came up to give him the once-over. Did we do it? *Bang!* A shell whizzes past the conning-tower the moment it showed above. *Whizz! bang!* they pitched all round while we wigwagged signals. That bird's eyes were so blinded by the combined glitter of fame and prize money he couldn't see anything, just then, but his own name in letters an inch high across the tops of five hundred million papers. Finally the skipper gives it up.
> 'Well,' he says, in his quiet way, 'if that bird don't want to recognize us, I don't know any way to make him. There's nothing left but to beat it.' Which we did, leaving him to go swelling into port with the tale of another U-boat sunk.

All the boats of the flotilla have had contests with the enemy, and later in the evening the commander told about his particular experience:

We'd heard Fritz for some time, and when his screws stopped, we came up to take a peep, and saw him lying dead on the water less than a mile away. There was nothing to it but to sneak up and shoot a 'fish' into him, and while we were making our approach according to Hoyle I felt all of an undertaker's proprietary rights in a funeral. He was mine; all over but the obsequies. But—oh, those 'buts'!—just as we started, the smoke of two destroyers shoved up on the horizon and scared the obsequies away. We love our little brother the destroyer, we do.

Hard luck, all right, (he accepted my condolences). But another commander of ours had worse. With a line shot, easy distance, he lost his bird through the torpedo exploding prematurely a few yards short of the mark. Fritz dived, of course, and the disappointment almost killed our chap. It actually made him physically ill. He didn't get over it for a deuce of a time.

One would imagine that it might. Subseas life is trying enough without the addition of such first class disappointments. For sheer grit and endurance under strain, the story of the passage of our "subs" from the United States to Europe is seldom surpassed, for they encountered a storm so violent that it almost sank the mother ship, a fine new vessel at that. The seas ran so high that she was lifted, quite often, and sat up on the peak of a wave with bows and stern both out of water; and when she dropped she would come down with a thump heavy enough to shake her to bits. As for the "subs"—they were blown like feathers in a north wind all over the ocean.

One boat was rolled till her compass fell out of its bearings, and four of them never saw each other or the tender again. Naturally, they had to economize on water, and for three weeks their crews never washed. All that time they were trying to get themselves reported. But when they would try to hail a ship, she would crack on her last knot and go flying like a scared chicken over the horizon, with funnels smoking like a house afire. They never did get themselves reported: were about given up for lost when, one at a time, they came straggling into harbour.

Three weeks without a wash! Think of it, my over-scrubbed fellow citizens, when, tonight, you crawl between cool white sheets in a ventilated bedroom. Think of *your* fellow citizen, the submariner, carrying on under the conditions herein set forth in order that Europe may have its bread for breakfast and your war taxes come to an end the sooner.

It has been my fortune, during the last year, to sojourn in a flooded front-line trench. I have cruised with every section of our fleet—destroyers, armed yachts, transports, chasers, mine layers and sweepers; have flown twelve hours and a half with the naval and military aviators of our twin services. But their work, soldiers and sailors, is at least carried on in the free air under sun and sky, while our friend the submariner—as wet as the trenches, as dangerous as the air service, subject to the same discomforts and dangers as the destroyers, with the added risks of subseas navigation plus war dangers—carries on in semi-darkness and impure air in the gloomy vaults of the sea.

It takes the strongest kind of man, physically and spiritually, to stand up under the strain. Hypothetically, the crews are supposed to have a week's rest after each cruise; but this particular hypothesis has been knocked bally west by the war along with a good many others. In order that their boat may go out on time and maintain its record for continuous service, many a crew works half of its prize days in port and far into the nights. You will find no slackers among the submariners. Cheerfully, uncomplainingly, they stand up under a grind that breaks down their machines, quoting in moments of severer stress the submariner's slogan:

It's a fine life—if you don't weaken.

And they understand. "We are being worked like dogs," one lad put it. "But so are the others—destroyers, chasers, yachts, battleships. It's the war. In peace times submarining isn't a bad job."

Also, they are doing valuable work. Thanks to them, Fritz can no longer bask on the surface in the sunlight and free air till the masts of a convoy poke above the horizon, for he never knows when an Allied "sub" may throw a "fish" into his solar plexus. During the daylight hours he must lie below; or, if obliged to come up, he must begin zizagging at once and so waste precious fuel in unnecessary mileage. Also he loses time. Subseas navigation is slow work. If you run more than two or three knots an hour, you quickly exhaust your batteries, and it takes hours of surface cruising to recharge them. An hour at full speed submerged will completely exhaust them.

It therefore takes Fritz longer, now, to come and go from his hunting-grounds, shortens his cruise, doubles his hardships by increased submergence. His life, never a happy one, has become insupportable, thanks to the Allied submarine. Dogged by patrols, bombed by seaplanes and "blimps," depth-mined by destroyers, voyaging always through a maze of nets and mines, he is now hunted underseas by huge steel sharks of his own kind. When Fritz comes to write his side of the underseas war, he will have some nasty things to say about Allied submarines.

CHAPTER 8

Our Toy Dreadnaughts

This is the saga of the toy dreadnaughts, the redoubtable "Tin Fleet" that sailed out of Hampton Roads, in 1917, to pick up the glove of defiance cast on the world's waters by Fritz of the submarines.

They had not been designed for such uses. Their wealth of polished teak and mahogany and glittering brass would have blinded the skipper of an ocean tramp. Their cabins were luxurious *boudoirs* for the pretty women and children they carried in summer weather up and down Long Island Sound. Until, like the black bursting of a typhoon, the war swept them into its seething caldron, their snowy decks had known no harder usage than the patter of little feet dancing under canopies of coloured lanterns. Up to the moment that Uncle Sam stretched out his lean, sinewy hand and gathered them in, they were merely millionaires' pleasure baubles.

We common folk who never have any money of our own love to picture our plutocrats as notorious money-grabbers without conscience or patriotism. When asked to lease their yachts, we knew just how they would behave—how they would gouge him for all he was worth. So just listen to the shameful way in which they behaved.

Take, for instance, the owner of the yacht in which I cruised recently in French waters. He happens to be vice-president of one of New York's largest banks—therefore the king robber of them all. Well, not only did he lease the yacht to the United States for the enormous sum of one dollar a year, but he spent thousands of his own good dollars fitting her for service. For two weeks a sacrilegious gang of ship's carpenters hammered spikes into the cabin mahogany, fitting it with bunks for the crew. Nor is the worth of his sacrifice diminished by the fact that it had all to be torn out again—for naval commanders have ideas of their own. The morning after Uncle Sam acquired the yacht, a

53

perfectly ruthless captain turned loose a perfectly shameless crew with pickaxes, and when the shades of evening closed on their labours, five car-loads of fancy woodwork lay on the deck. Stripped like a boxer for action, guns bolted to her decks, depth-mines poised astern, she led the "Suicide Fleet"—so named by those who watched it go—out of Hampton Roads.

A baker's dozen of tin toy yachts going to war? It did seem ridiculous—like some other famous ventures. Against one German raider they would have stood about the same chance as Leif Ericsson's galley or the *pinta* of Columbus—and they were just about as big. It seemed, almost, that any respectable war vessel that happened to meet them *en route* would "pinch" them, as a policeman picks up a lost child, and lead them back to their mother ship. But they sailed on, and, with the exception of an occasional paragraph in the papers, were lost to view in the war fogs that blanket European waters. Unseen, unheralded, unheard of, ignoring that modern eleventh commandment which reads, "*Give us this day our daily ad,*" that "tin toy fleet" carried on in the performance of an amazing duty.

What did it do? Well, as we all know, the winning of the war is altogether dependent upon the ability of the Allies to maintain sea communications. Germany acknowledged this when she chose war with the United States rather than abandon unrestricted submarine war. She knew that all she had to do was to stop us and them from delivering in Europe our armies, the supplies to maintain them; also the vast war material contributed by Canada, ourselves, Central and South Americas, the Pacific Isles, New Zealand, Australia, Africa, and all that Asian trade which comes around the Cape of Good Hope. All of this enormous aggregation of shipping, probably nine tenths of all the world owns, passes through a triangle the base of which extends from Canada to Cape Horn and which has its apex in a "bottle neck" a hundred miles wide between Ireland and Cape Ushant. Through that neck ten thousand ships pass in and out each week.

It was this fact that caused the Germans to establish submarine bases at Ostend and Zeebrügge. The U-boats could be brought through the Bruges Canal from Germany, and so shot through the bottle neck into the thick of Allied shipping. It was this fact that underlay the strategy of the British in their successful attempt to thrust a cork into the neck of the bottle. Not for nothing did nearly six hundred British sailors give their lives. Not only did their sacrifice set the German U-boat bases back three hundred miles, and force them to use their old outlets into the North Sea, but it freed for active service against the submarines half a hundred destroyers of the Dover patrol, which for three years had stood guard to prevent the "tip and run" raids of German destroyers. Lastly, the new mine area just declared by the British Admiralty has almost blocked the North Sea outlets. Only with great difficulty will the U-boats now be able to make their way through closely guarded channels.

A good many people, perhaps most people, have held the erroneous belief that, because our fleets were operating south of England and Ireland, far from the North Sea, the waters in which they were operating were comparatively safe. This is exactly contrary to the truth. Before our destroyers and the "tin fleet" were turned into it to help the British out, the bottle neck was the U-boats' happy hunting-ground. Through it go three main lines of our transports and supply ships, escorted by the "tin fleet" to their docks in French ports. In addition, the baker's dozen of them, assisted by a brace of obsolete destroyers, have escorted large convoys up and down the French coast, and the quality and quantity of their work may be gaged by the fact that the U-boats have bagged only two out of nearly thirty thousand. Quietly, efficiently, as is the Navy way, they played a large part in the most remarkable transportation problem of all time.

J. P. Morgan's famous yacht *Corsair*
Later in service of the U. S. Navy as scout cruiser

DECK OF A U. S. TORPEDO BOAT DESTROYER
IN FRENCH WATERS
This shows how the decks are cleared for action while
the destroyer is acting as a guard for our transports

CHAPTER 9

Our First Line of Defence

A comparison will make this clear. When the Japanese threw their armies into Manchuria, their lines of communication were the longest on record. Their total force in the field, however, never exceeded four hundred thousand. The British lines in the South African war were still longer; but their army numbered little more than half that of the Japanese, and they enjoyed the advantage of a local base. But, with armies already twice as large as that of the Japanese, and which may be ten times as large, our lines of communication are longer than those of the British. From California to France, more than seven thousand miles, our extreme line extends. Not a man or a horse or a gun or a pound of supplies moves less than four thousand miles in transit to the front; and, whereas the Japanese and British lines were unmenaced by their foes, oars are constantly exposed to U-boat attacks. And here it is that the "tin fleet" takes hold.

Working in conjunction with our destroyer flotilla in English waters, it picks up transports and supply ships on the outer edge of the submarine zone, and convoys them safely into port, interposing its own *papier-mâché* bulwarks between them and attack. Also—and this is equally important, for a ship's bottom is as valuable empty as full—it escorts them back to the ocean door; sees them, as it were, across the yard and past the dog. In fact, the "tin fleet" forms our first battle-line—the real American front, on which Americans were killing Boches and being killed before the first soldier left our shores: a fact that was not so clearly established in my mind as it ought to have been when I called on its Admiral for the first time.

His eyes flashed under straight gray brows when I spoke of an approaching visit to the "American front." "You are there now," he said, with quiet that emphasized the fact. "Take a cruise with us and you'll soon find it out." I did. An hour later saw me walking with one of his captains down to the boat wharf. The port at which the fleet bases is said to have been founded by the Phoenicians. This is quite believable, for it is easy to see that its narrow streets follow the meanderings of those first world mariners over the hills on Sunday jaunts with early Breton maids; and, as sailor nature never changes, our lads now follow in their footsteps with the Bretons' feminine descendants.

The grim *chateau* that looks in its stone embrace, on an inner boat harbour, is credited, on the other hand, to Julius Caesar, who sailed his galleys therefrom to the conquest of Britain. It took those stubborn English three hundred years to cast off the yoke he placed on their necks, but they did it at last Now, some fifteen hundred years later, I was ferried out of its stone portals by their lineal descendants, again at war with a power whose dreams of world conquest transcend a Caesar's maddest visions. National paranoia, like history, appears to run in cycles.

Long before we reached them, my gaze went to three yachts that lay at anchor under the lea of a long breakwater. They did look small. But, just as a little man's courage adds to his inches, so their performance in the past year caused them to loom in my sight large as battle-ships. When, stepping aboard, I noted the guns fore and aft, the quick firers on the boat-deck above, the nest of depth-mines astern, I realized the secret of the "tin fleet's" power: they could not be more effective if fired from a ship half a mile long.

The officers and crew were as remarkable as their ship. Only the captain was an Annapolis man. The others, from the Naval Reserve, counted a stock broker, a bond clerk, a Staten Island Ferry engineer, a Montana cattleman, and others. All were following the pursuits of peace when we went into the war. One, I believe, had never seen the ocean before he went on board. Yet now, after a year's study backed by arduous practical applications, they were all capable officers.

The crew was still more astonishing. Fully a third of the men before the mast were Harvard, Yale, or Princeton students, scions of America's wealthiest families, shipped for the "duration"—said "duration," as one of them put it, being "like the indeterminate sentences the judges pass on you nowadays—you stay in as long as you're good." One quartermaster, a man over forty years of age, was once tax commissioner of New Jersey and had served two terms in its State legislature. It was quite startling to hear the cultivated college speech issuing from a group of tarry sailors who were heaving up anchor forward.

Indeed, the yacht might easily have furnished a *motif* for one of those musical comedies in which an admiral is "shanghaied" and shipped before the mast in a vessel manned by chorus girls. She needed only to pick up a torpedoed heroine and an unprincipled adventurer to go right into the "movies."

Apart from this possible plot, there is little comedy aboard the yacht. Hard work and hard weather have been the daily fare of these lads brought up to luxury, and they have thriven on it. Tall, straight, and strong, they are as fine a lot of sailormen as ever hauled upon a rope. The anchor apeak, they hoisted the depth-mines into position astern, set the time machinery, shotted the guns. Ready for war, the yacht picked her way through the shipping to pick up a Channel convoy in the outer harbour.

Before we sailed, the skippers of all the ships and two French pilots came aboard for a conference, representatives of almost all the Allied and neutral marines. Not a man of them but had been torpedoed once, some more than once; yet, quiet, ordinary-looking men, to whom you would never have accorded a second glance on the street, they were still pursuing the path of duty through those dangerous seas. They accepted with little nods their places in convoy; listened quietly to the captain's directions in case of attack to beat it—for all they were worth while the yachts laid down a depth-mine barrage between them and the U-boats. Not till he spoke of fog, more dreaded by convoys than the U-boat, did the worry that dogs their footsteps day and night make itself felt.

"Let's hope that won't be added to our troubles," said one.

Another added: "We've enough as it is."

Quiet, unheroic, commonplace, prosaic; quieter than children in church; commonplace as the baker who sells you your bread. Yet, the more powerfully because their appearance was so badly out of key with the glowing romance of war, one felt the sinister dangers amid which they live. The life history of any one of those prosaic skippers would out-thrill a Dumas romance.

I am in position to write one chapter: which began when, next morning, fog caught us in a dangerous passage between shore and shoals and rolled us up in a thick gray blanket. A heavy sea gave us a miserable roll, and I was trying to sleep off some seasick qualms in the cabin below when the screws stopped, then went full speed astern.

When that happens in the submarine zone, you don't stand on the order of your going—you simply go! I went up on deck in three hops—just in time to see the fog roll back like a theatre curtain from a tall tower uprising from a smother of foam. It takes time to stop a ship's headway, and for a couple of minutes it was an open question whether or not we should bump that perfectly good French lighthouse off the map. We were closer than any of us liked before she began to back off, and some of the others were not so lucky.

It seems that the French pilot on the leading ship had made his turn to go around the lighthouse a bit too soon, and he was on the beach. Another, one of the new steel standardized ships, had bumped over a reef with only a little damage to her bottom. But that was not the end. The other ships now came driving on through the fog, and mixed in a *mêlée*, dodging, tacking, backing, wilder than a madhouse *cotillion*. One just missed our bows. A second passed astern. For a while anything might have happened; but, as though impatient to view his evil work, the fog demon lifted the edge of his gray curtain in the nick of time. As though realizing his mistake, he hastily dropped it again. But we had seen each other in the clear. The tangle straightened out into columns again—that is, as close to columns as merchant skippers can get.

They never keep mathematically correct line and distance, like Navy men, and the short-comings of our present lot in this respect caused much strafing on the bridge and kept a dazzle of flags at work translating it into the politer language of the naval code. When removed from the rear to the head of his column, one persistent laggard reminded me of a stout lady in a Californian talking club, who "groused" at the pace till she herself was placed in the lead; whereafter she almost walked the legs off her companions. After he moved ahead, it took all the flags in the signal-box to prevent our laggard from running right out of sight. Returning to the mix-up in the fog, it was one of those haps that occur to all convoys and are responsible for a grizzle of gray on heads that left our shores a year ago flying the full colours of youth. Leaving one yacht with the stranded ship,—which backed off at high tide,—we sailed on toward a point which was said to be the headquarters of a German submarine.

A red pin with a date under it only a day old marked its last reported position on the bridge chart. A scattering of others indicated more U-boats, but the dates under those were older; for, with the assistance of the hydroplane and "blimp" patrols, Uncle Sam has established the entire length of the French coast, the yachts have made those waters exceedingly unhealthy for submarines. A devil's spawning of mines in the ship's channels at night is about the limit of their present attempts.

Just before the fog entirely cleared away, a radio had warned us away from a certain channel where the lone pirate of the point had evidently put in a good night's work. But his labours went for naught. Across our bows, a fleet of mine-sweepers swept in swift procession to clear away his infernal litter. While they were still in sight two hydroplanes came booming like great bumble-bees out from the land to escort us across their forty-mile sector. Thus, in one view, were grouped the three American services that render commerce possible in these seas.

The hydroplanes had a special interest for me, because I had flown with them on patrol only a few weeks before, and had taken photographs from above of those very yachts. At that time submarines were shy as quail at the end of the open season, and our flying sailors a spell of silence even on the sailor lads who were skylarking astern. Over the ship fell a hush that was broken only by the heartbeat of the screw.

"Yachting in the Mediterranean." The officer on the bridge broke the long silence. "This is what your millionaire pays his good money for."

In our case it was literally true; for our boat, a converted yacht in the Mediterranean fleet of the United States, was said before the war to be the finest yacht in the world. Then she was a sailor's dream of polished wood, brass, and copper, her decks snow-white from a daily bleach of squeezed lemons. It spoiled a million dollars a year to keep her in commission and entertain the princes, presidents, and kings who used her for a playground.

Generally she lay at Kiel, and one of her officers possesses an engraved card of invitation to the great annual ball after the Kiel Regatta, signed by His Imperial Majesty the *Kaiser*. Another American officer occupies the beautiful stateroom in which the *Kaiser* often slept, and the steward who used to wait upon him was still on board when the yacht was taken into government service. He told many an interesting story of the days when the *Kaiser* and King Edward sat at opposite ends of the ward-room table now used—the irony of events!—by American officers busily engaged in hunting down His Imperial Majesty's U-boats. He said that the *Kaiser* appeared to be very fond of his uncle—which affords a revealing glimpse of his character; for we know that even in those days he was plotting to enslave the world and bind England with German-forged chains.

While we stood on the bridge talking, some of His Imperial Majesty's latest work went floating by in the shape of torpedoed wreckage; and as the sky glow passed through every shade of crimson and rose to deepest saffron, and the sea's violet deepened to indigo, my companion laid before me the problem of the Mediterranean.

Conditions here are ideal for U-boat operations. The Mediterranean is a bottle two thousand miles in length, with a neck at each end, and squeezed thin in the middle between Sicily and the African coast. Through the bottle neck at Gibraltar at one end, the Suez Canal at the other, passes a large trade. To understand its volume, just draw a line from Canada to Gibraltar; another from Cape Horn. Into that great triangle pours not only the trade of the Americas and the Panama Canal, but into it, also, comes the West African trade from the south; the British, French, and Scandinavian from the north; all of the world's trade for the far East and those dozen nations that have sea borders along the Mediterranean. After passing in at Gibraltar, this stream of ships cannot diverge very widely; for, though, as you know, we are a day's sail from Gib., Africa and Spain are both in sight. And the stream must concentrate again between Sicily and Africa. This makes good hunting for U-boats. They have two fat chances, coming and going, at every ship.

The neutrality of Spain, again, favours the U-boats—though not to the extent one might suppose. It is true they can, and no doubt do, obtain fresh food supplies from Spanish fisher-men. The length of a U-boat's cruise, however, is not determined by fuel or food. Of these she carries sufficient for the longest cruise. But when her torpedoes and ammunition are exhausted, she must return to her base at Pola or Cattaro in the Adriatic. Spain's chief use to the U-boat is as a city or refuge to which it can fly from immediate pursuit, or intern if badly damaged.

Lastly, when Germany threw a strangler's cord of U-boats around the British Isles in a desperate attempt to throttle her commerce, it took every sailor and ship England could muster to keep her own ports open and Germany's closed. After we came into the war, it became still more necessary to guard the American transport lines. Accordingly, the fastest and best ships were naturally used for that service, leaving less important areas to be guarded by slower boats.

CHAPTER 12

A Remarkable Fleet

I had already seen our fleet perhaps the most remarkable that was ever swept together by a strenuous emergency. Add to a score of converted yachts half a dozen Coast Guard vessels; a few old destroyers; a couple of ice-breakers drawn from service in Northern harbours; a gunboat built especially for use on Chinese rivers, with cigarette funnels almost as tall as her masts; a vessel that fired the first gun in the Spanish-American war; mix well, and throw in a seasoning of "chasers" and submarines, and you have our Mediterranean fleet. Of the destroyers, one had lain at the bottom of the ocean for six months, and would have been there yet if the dire need for ships had not caused her resurrection. Most of the others had served for years in the Philippines, under orders never, never, *never* to venture beyond swimming distance from the land. It is said, indeed, that a machinist's mate was tried by general court-martial for inadvertently dropping a monkey-wrench through one ship's bottom; but, though this, perhaps, ought to be taken as a figure of speech, it conveys a fair idea of their condition when the war came along and knocked the doctrine of safety first into a cocked hat.

Half way round the world, through the China and Indian seas, they had come by way of Suez, meeting some savage weather on the way. From a few stray observations, I gathered that the trip must have been quite Homeric. But, when cross-examined, all their commander could remember was that he had "bought the finest lace you ever saw at Malta." However, such as they are, here they are, setting the pace for the Coast Guard.

Between the latter service and the Navy, by the way, exists an ancient rivalry, which is expressed in a saying:

When the Navy runs for port, the Coast Guard puts to sea!

The feeling undoubtedly bases in pride of ancestry: for your true blue Coast Guardsman proudly traces his lineage back to Noah, who ran the Ark on the first patrol around the peak of Ararat. His service, he asserts, was quite mildewed with age before the "upstart Navy" put to sea in the first basket coracle calked with clay. The Navy, on the other hand, holds the Coast Guard in tolerance as a sort of hybrid, half animal, half fish—a composite between a lighthouse-keeper and a revenue shark. Nevertheless, here Coast Guard and Navy have fused so completely that it is impossible to tell where one leaves off and the other begins.

Working in perfect harmony, they are getting results; for not a boat of them—ice-breakers, ramshackle destroyers, China steamers, yachts—is averaging less than four thousand steaming miles a month. The yacht under my feet had done her fifty-six hundred in the last thirty days—twice the distance between Liverpool and New York.

Blow high, blow low, they ran their convoys last winter through black night rains, bitter frosts, dreaded fogs, half the length of the Mediterranean, and from the Strait of Gibraltar fourteen hundred miles northward to British and French ports: for the stream of ships, the Allies' arterial blood, must be kept in circulation.

A radio exchange between one yacht and her consort during a Biscay storm eloquently explains that hard winter's work:

I am in sinking condition. Please stand by to help.

To which the other replied:

Am sinking myself.

Both were awash below, about due to founder, when a sudden break in the storm saved them.

The record of lives lost last winter also tells the tale of hardship and danger—of American lives paid to insure the delivery of Allied supplies. The converted yacht *Alcedo*, torpedoed in French waters; the destroyer *Jacob Jones*, sunk by the U-53 in the English Channel; the *Chauncey*, with a loss of life of over one hundred, were part of the price. From other ships twenty-two men were washed overboard and drowned; and many others have had marvellous escapes.

One lad, washed overboard in a black night storm, was thought to be hopelessly lost till a voice hailed the watch from under the stern. He had caught the log-line, which trails a couple of hundred feet behind, and hauled himself along it.

Another escape was still more marvellous. Washed overboard at night from a destroyer, this particular lad was heaved by a wave on to the deck of another vessel half a mile astern. When restored to his own ship at the end of the voyage, his captain thus addressed him:

Young man, you have used up all the luck you will have in all your life. The Navy is no safe place for you. Take my advice— get out of it as soon as Uncle Sam will let you.

CHAPTER 13

A Night Watch on the Bridge

There is nothing like a night watch on the bridge to produce stories. The quiet and darkness, broken only by the heart-beat of the screw timing the lap of the waves under the bows, provides the ideal atmosphere. One has only to listen to have the whole underseas war unroll like a cinema on the night's warm curtain. My companion had spent an evening before we left port with the commander of the British E-boat that sank the German "super-submarine" off Cape St. Vincent, and now he told it to me just as it had been given to him:

It wasn't really a super-submarine, though the reports all gave it as that. It was really a bigger sub of the *Deutschland* type. In fact, the 'undersea cruiser' the Hun has talked so much about has not yet appeared. Nevertheless, it was some bag, and the 'Limey' skipper deserves all the credit he got, for he trailed the critter seventeen hours.

He ran into the Hun's wake at daybreak. It was a fine, clean wake, so he knew the U-boat couldn't be far ahead; but it was late afternoon before he got his first sight. After that he manoeuvred four hours more for position and smoked fifty cigarettes before, at dusk, he got the Hun between him and the sunset, so close that she bulked like a dark island against the smouldering sky.

She was dead ahead, and so near that he could see men walking up and down her deck, enjoying the cool of the evening. As he said: 'She was mine. God himself couldn't have taken her from me.' He watched her for a full minute. Then—he gave her one fish in the bows, another astern. She heaved up like a stricken whale, and sank in a cloud of smoke.

It was a vivid picture he had drawn—the long, dark hulk against the sunset sky; a tremendous explosion; the dark waves closing over the place she had been. *He who lives by the sword shall perish by the sword,* the Scriptures tell us. The retribution that overtakes these Hun commanders is swifter than the lightning when it strikes. "He gave her one fish in the bows, another astern. She sank in a cloud of smoke."

The executive officer had joined us while we were talking. Now he put in:

Did you hear of the two U-boats that were sunk coming through the Straits? It was the more important because it settles beyond doubt the question as to whether their base at Zeebrügge was really plugged. They had been cruising in the Bay of Biscay, and received wireless orders not to attempt to return to Zeebrügge, but to proceed to the Mediterranean and base at Pola. Just how the British found it out, I don't know. Moreover, it is none of our business. The point is—they knew just when to expect those subs. One midnight they were detected coming through the Straits, were followed, and two out of three sunk. There hasn't been so much rejoicing at the base since they sank old 'Spartel Jack.'

Every base has some Hun commander who has achieved notoriety—usually by differing from the bloody practices of his fellows. In Irish waters it has been "Kelly," the one man who fought like a gentleman. In French waters, "Penmarsh Pete" was the celebrated local character—though his reputation was due to an oyster-like clinging to the rock after which he was named, and his industry in sowing a devil's spawn of mines between dusk and dark in the French ship-channels. Now I heard of "Spartel Jack," who held the limelight in the Mediterranean.

Like "Kelly," "Spartel" was a fair fighter, and always warned his ships before sinking them; and, if it was not practicable to tow the boats to land himself, he would wireless their position in to the base. His boat was finally crippled so badly by a depth-bomb that he had to intern at a Spanish port; whereupon a number of 'Limeys' donned civilian clothes and went up to see her. Lo and behold! who should they recognize in "Jack" but an old acquaintance, tugboat captain who had served twelve years at the base before the war. He greeted them nicely, but "grouched" a bit about his internment. He had never liked Spanish cooking! And when the news spread, and more old friends came up to see him, "Jack" was gone. He had provided the world with another Hun scandal by breaking internment.

Thereafter the old pirate carried on with his sinkings until, not long ago, a depth-mine sent his boat to the bottom. But he did not go with her; for, just as she sank, the hatch flew up and two men leaped out. One was "Jack"—so badly injured, however, by the explosion, that he died a few days later in the base hospital—greatly to the regret of the British, who love a game enemy.

His passing, however, was attended by one of those tragedies that cross-cut all underseas stories. Three English captains, whom "Jack" was just about ready to take back to Germany, are said to have gone down with his boat.

Genuine human feeling, the despised "human interest" of the high-brow critic, crops up in many stories. Man that is born of woman must have something to love, and, in lieu of their wives, sisters, and sweethearts, sailors' affections usually centre on some dumb animal— preferably a dog.

A boat of castaways, picked up by our yacht, had with them a fine hound bitch that had just given birth to two pups when the ship was torpedoed. One pup was killed by the explosion; but the sailors wrapped the mother and surviving pup in a pea-jacket, and placed them in the boat. But when, hours later, the coat was opened, instead of one, four wiggly puppies raised their heads for a first blink at their mother's world. She, poor creature, died. Whereupon the crew adopted the orphans and brought them up on a bottle. They can still hardly toddle, but their hundred and seven foster-fathers are ready to bet a year's pay as to their ability to whip their weight in kittens.

While the tales were in course, a brilliant tropic moon had sailed up from behind Africa, and now laid a silver finger upon a mass of floating wreckage: the second reminder that evening of the danger that dogs the heels of the fleet. Thoughts of the torpedo that might come crashing at any moment through the side accompanied me down to my stateroom. When the *Alcedo* was torpedoed, at night, her wireless operator was blown out of his bunk through the deck—and, with great presence of mind, ran straight to his post and began to tick off an S. O. S. I remembered it, and fell asleep with a death grip on the sides of my bed, intending the deck and ceiling beams to be well out of my way before I rose.

CHAPTER 14

Africa!

I gained the deck next morning, however, in the customary manner, to find the convoy steaming through golden sunlight across a bright blue sea. A dirigible that had just come over from Africa soared above, all silver iridescence. It guarded us the greater part of the day, and when it left, a hydroplane came booming like a great insect out from the land, to circle and recircle the convoy. Others appeared during the remaining three days of our voyage along those pleasant seas; nor left us long alone till we dropped anchor in the harbour of an African port.

With its mosques and *minarets*, narrow streets which meandered at will under frequent arches into all sorts of blind alleys, guts and pockets, it was about as queer a corner of the world as any into which the war has pitched our sailor-boys. Through narrow, barred windows one caught the dark flash of Oriental eyes. Veiled women shuffled past in twos and threes. Within recessed doorways, wonderfully nailed in strange patterns, old Arabs in flowing white *burnouses* smoked and drank in stately calm that took no heed of the war or civilization's frets.

Sitting, that evening, with the ship's doctor under the portals of a *café*, I watched the white sailor caps of our boys go bobbing down a polyglot human stream in which the horizon-blue tunics and crimson breeches of the French, English brass and khaki, red and yellow of negroid troops, and various uniforms of Italians and Serbians formed a brilliant setting around the white background of Arab garments. Their bright, clean American faces shone still brighter and cleaner by comparison with the muddy brown visages around them. Cheerful, good-natured, they floated along the human stream, or sat in groups sipping the warm native beer.

To us, sitting there, came one of our ensigns with three "Limey" officers in tow, commanders of patrol-boats serving with our squadron, than whom the war has produced no braver or hardier set of men. And while that stream of humanity flowed like liquid fire under our eyes, fluxing and flowing in new colour combinations, they talked ship talk that was at once both history and romance.

One had served in the North Sea at the beginning of the war, and he told, with a queer little grin, of his experiences:

At first we had nothing but a three-pound pop-gun to chase Fritz off the waters—and him carrying three-inch guns. On his part, Fritz wasn't gunning for small game like us; so, without any *pourparlers* or conversations, we arrived at a mutual understanding to keep out of each other's way. He didn't bother us unless we interfered with a sinking; then he'd chase us.

After we got real guns, of course, we went after him—war to the knife. If he saw us first, that ended it—for us. If it was the other way, up he'd go in spray and smoke—unless your gunner got rattled, like ours did one day. Fritz had come up less than five hundred yards away—close enough for a woman to hit him with a potato; and we were already beginning to count the prize money, when *bang!* went our first gun.

That shell is going yet. The next plumped into the water half way. The third didn't miss by more than half a mile. And no doubt, if Fritz had been so obliging as to stand still, we might have got him during the day. But about that time he got busy and threw a torpedo into our stern.

Up went our depth-mines, of course. The stern gun was blown fully two hundred feet up in the air. I can see it now, sailing like a bird, carriage and all, and looking so darned funny that I laughed out loud. It was really what you writer chaps call a tragic situation, for we were all due to die, and I wouldn't have believed anything funny could come out of it. But when I saw the skipper shaking his fist in the face of that fool gunner, I had to laugh again.

'You son-of-a-gun!' he yelled. 'Is this why the British government paid two hundred pounds for your education—to shoot up the firmament and plug holes in the sea? If you weren't due to drown in five minutes, I'd brain you myself. But drown you will, damn you, along with the rest of us.'

He said it! Just then a second torpedo took us in the bows, and sent him, the gun and gunner, up in the air together. The ship just melted; and when things quit raining down, I found myself with the ship's boy clinging to a piece of a deckhouse. About a dozen of the crew were floating among the wreckage, and we had scarcely got the water out of our eyes before the U-boat came shooting down through us, so close that we could see the commander's eyes as he leaned down from the conning-tower. 'How's the water?' he called in good English.

'Cold,' the man nearest him answered. 'Aren't you going to pick us up?'

He shook his head. 'No. The devil's been waiting for you chaps a damned long time. You'll be warm enough pretty soon. You will all be in hell for breakfast.'

He sailed past, then circled and came tearing back, trying to drown us with his wash. Time and again he did it, and churned up somebody with his screws. The boy and I had drifted out to the edge, and were hanging as low as possible in the water; for already I had sighted smoke on the horizon, and was sure if the Hun saw it he'd machine-gun us right there in the water. But he didn't think it worth his while. The last time he charged through, he swung his thumb over his shoulder.

'Friend of mine out yonder. I'll have to go. Sorry I can't stay and see your finish. But it won't be long. You'll all be drowned before that chap gets up.'

Most of us were; for during the two hours it took the patrol-boat to come up, the men chilled in that frozen North Sea water, and let go, till none were left but me and the boy. He had stuck it out like a little brick; but now he tried to give in.

'We're going to drown anyway,' he said, 'so what's the use of suffering! I'm going to let go and get it over with.'

I couldn't have stopped him, for I was all in myself; but I put up a good bluff: 'Just try it, you little devil! I'll swim around and tie you there, and skin you raw with a rope's end after I get you on board.' And it worked, for he hung on till we were picked up.

This was one of a dozen similar stories that passed around the table: all dramatic, all on the raw edge of life, where shams and illusions are stripped away and nothing left but fundamentals. While they talked I learned more of the under seas war than one could pick up in a couple of years of actual service; for they were experts, wise in the way of the U-boats. It was they who divided the seafarers for me into two great classes—merchant sailors, the hunted; the U-boats, the hunters; the one just as much the prey of the other as is the deer of the tiger. And the more I heard of the hunters, the more I wondered at the quiet heroism of the hunted.

"Dipped" is their careless slang for being torpedoed. At the base I had met men who had been "dipped" two, three, four times. One holds the record with nine torpedoings, and emerges each time like a hard-shell Baptist, confirmed in his faith. Though profane, his profession is nevertheless founded on the highest order of patriotism:

To hell with the U-boats! They can't keep me off the sea.

Another thing I learned. Just as the air service has its stars, so the underseas war has developed crack commanders on both sides who are known to each other. To "get" one of the big fellows lifts a green commander at once into the ranks of the stars, and the desire to do it has caused many a daring hazard.

One German commander—a real Hun, for he was a Prussian baron—sent a challenge by the crew of a ship he had torpedoed to an English E-boat man. As in duty bound, the English-man submitted the letter to his admiral, who promptly refused permission. It is said, however, that the commander received orders, next day, that would take his vessel across the position stated in the Prussian's letter at the hour named. Also, rumour has it that the admiral sat in the radio room till he received the following message:

While proceeding according to orders, encountered a German U-boat. Sank him.

The details of this desperate duel would be mighty interesting; but it is doubtful whether they will ever be heard beyond the confines of the place where real naval history is taught—the bars where sailormen congregate.

CHAPTER 15

A Sea Duel

We sat so late that night, we were already at sea when I came on deck next morning, with a new convoy zigzagging on our beam. The return voyage was quite uneventful. The few submarines mentioned in the "Allos" were far away. Seamen are great believers in luck, and, because I had been present at the capture of the first German submarine by our flotilla in Irish waters, the entire ship's company had banked on me to produce another. Accordingly, as I sat with the ship's doctor on the deck the last morning at sea, an ensign asked in passing:

"Well, where's our submarine?" Now, it chanced that for the last hour we had been watching a smooth water-line that paralleled our course. We answered in concert: "There—at the end of that wake."

The ensign looked and laughed. "That's only a tide-slick."

We, however, remained unconvinced. Twice that day we thought we detected a yellowish oil gleam when our zigzags crossed its course. Nor were we mistaken; for a few hours later in came a radio from a merchantman about twenty miles ahead:

Submarine chasing me. Send help.

We replied telling him to hold out till we came up, and received a reply half an hour later:

Submarine shelling me from six thousand yards. Am replying to his fire.

Fine old merchantman! We radioed further encouragement while stoking our fires—on fire ourselves at the chance of getting that submarine. But it was not for us. Just as the sun sank, in a cloud glory of amber and gold, came the last message:

Have landed three shells on submarine at three thousand yards. It sank in cloud of smoke.

So Fritz does not have it all his own way, for many U-boats are sunk by fighting merchantmen. Neither do all the torpedoed ships reported by U-boat commanders go to the bottom. Many limp into port with severe injuries. One I saw in an African harbour had a hole in her side forty-two feet wide and twenty-seven high, broad and high enough to drive four trains through abreast. Holes twenty feet square are quite common, and many ships are either beached after being torpedoed, or go down in water so shallow that they are easily salvaged.

From January, 1915, to December, 1917, two hundred and sixty-seven ships were salvaged by the British in their home waters. But this year, owing to improved methods, one hundred and forty-seven ships were salvaged in five months. The French Minister of Marine told us recently that Allied tonnage restored to the sea by repaired ships has exceeded five hundred thousand tons weekly. In one week Great Britain repaired five hundred and ninety-eight thousand tons, while France restored two hundred and sixty thousand tons in one month. Some of these ships were brought up from depths of ninety feet; and the service, which is constantly becoming more efficient, is now being extended to foreign waters.

Neither do the omens in the Mediterranean portend good for Fritz. During my month there, three U-boats were sunk by the British alone, and a fourth was so badly crippled that it had to intern at a Spanish port; and, day by day, newer and swifter boats are being added to the Allied fleets.

Now that Zeebrügge is closed, indeed, Pola and Cattaro alone remain to be dealt with. Tactically, the problem is quite simple. At its mouth the Adriatic is only forty-five miles wide, and a chain of patrol-boats with guns, listening apparatus, and depth-mines is now stretched across it. Henceforth Fritz is going to find it very difficult to get out to his hunting-grounds; in fact, one of him was sunk trying it just the other day. Judging from the exclamation of a commander of ours who has still to get his "sub," Fritz's days in the Mediterranean are numbered.

"If we don't get a 'sub' this month—*goodnight!* They'll soon be scarce as orchids in Greenland."

In the meantime, he and his crew are carrying on with grim determination to "get" that "sub" before the season closes. Never have

I seen men keener, with a finer-tempered edge for the work. When half a dozen were left at an African port because of a hurry call that sent their ship after a submarine, they begged the commander of a French dirigible station to fly them out and drop them in the water near their ship.

There can be nothing more wearing to the spirit than persistent watching and waiting for an unseen attack. Yet it has not affected their morale. They go at the gun drills with a will. At almost any hour of the day a couple of lads may be seen with eyes glued to the telescopic sights, taking a little private practice.

Of course they grow weary. One evening I heard two of them reflecting invidiously on the Mediterranean ports. "Dirty holes," one said. "I'm scared to open my mouth in any of them, for fear of swallowing forty million germs."

"You bet!" the other answered. "The good old U. S. for me. It's the one clean spot on earth. When I once get back there—I'll stay put."

He meant it. Yet, when the tragic turmoil of this war passes, and he and his comrades look down the lengthening perspectives of time on the hot, fetid life of these African ports, when they see the long panorama of golden Spanish mountains and foothill towns unrolling again in memory, and recall the "Allos" and S. O. S., the wrecks, sinkings, U-boat duels, the splendid sunrises and settings over violet seas, the tropic moons sailing from dusky horizons to brilliant meridians, the loud tattoo of torrential rains on the deck, the sheet-lightnings that lift a ghost convoy out of an inky sea—when they look back on all this from the peace of prairie farms or mountain homesteads, they will see that to which their eyes are now blind: the angel of romance flying before them with roseate wings.

When occasion throws two of them together in the years to come, they will agree, with wise wags of the head:

Those were the good old days!

CHAPTER 16

Convoys and Submarines

Out in the harbour a thirty-vessel convoy was nosing up to its anchors. The hiss of steam and the rattle of the winches carried across the water and up the hill to where, from his office windows, the base Admiral watched the departure.

His gaze centred on one ship, a fine steamer, which, with her cargo of twelve thousand tons of meat, was worth fully three million dollars. Her potential values, however, far exceeded that figure: for the meat stood for human flesh—the flesh of women and children in France and England; for the thews and sinews of millions of soldiers who must be well fed if the world was to escape the German yoke.

The ship was commanded by a Scotch skipper, an admirable character, upright, courageous, self-reliant, the finest of seamen, but, unfortunately, hard in the mouth. Before the convoy system was established he had voyaged a score of times through the submarine zone, winning his way to safety by seamanship and daring. A torpedo had once shaved his bows. Another had almost clipped off his stern. He had fought half a dozen artillery battles and got away with it. All of which had raised his opinion of himself and his ship fairly close to omnipotence. He hated the naval discipline of convoys as much as their slow speed, and had bolted them twice. This fact was in the base Admiral's mind when he turned to his chief of staff:

McGregor, down there, has bolted twice. I have advised his owners to replace him, but they won't. Sooner or later, if he isn't stopped, the U-boats will get him, Radio N—— to watch him closely.

The order was duly noted by the senior commander of the destroyer group that escorted the convoy to sea, and when his executive officer reported a few hours later that McGregor was edging out of his column, the destroyer went after him like a dog charging a bolting sheep.

"Who do you think you are, anyway?" the commander "bawled him out" through the megaphone. "Try that again, and I'll put an officer on your bridge and recommend that your papers be cancelled."

"That ought to hold him," he remarked to his executive, as McGregor came back to line. "But I'll bet you the old chap is raving. His crew will need to step lively for the next few hours."

And raving McGregor surely was. If printed here his remarks, as afterward reported by his crew, would burn a hole in the page. He, a master of twenty years' standing, to be ordered about by a Yank! He had outfought, outwitted, outrun more U-boats than the entire American flotilla had seen in the course of its operations! He, with a sixteen-knot ship, to be held down to an eight-knot crawl! Put an officer on his bridge, would they? Cancel his papers, hey? And so forth, with profuse marginal notes and profane trimmings.

If a plausible excuse, in the shape of a fog that fell like a thick gray blanket over the convoy, had not been furnished these fulminations, no doubt, would presently have subsided. He would hardly have dared violate such specific orders. But when the fog lifted toward evening, the convoy was scattered over the seas to the horizon, and came scuttering back like frightened chickens in response to the destroyers' radio cluckings—all but McGregor, who was out of sight. Next news of him came in an agonized call from a point just over the horizon:

I'm torpedoed! Sinking! Submarine shelling boats! Come at once!

Too late! On the wide and lonely ocean that had just engulfed that fine ship with her sorely needed food, the potential flesh of thousands, they found two shell-torn boats full of wounded and dying men.

In the crestfallen, troubled man who sat in their midst it were difficult to recognize the old hard-mouth who had raved on his bridge a few hours before. He was repentant, of course; but the tears that squeezed out of his hard eyes could not restore that fine ship or heal the wounds of his crew. From one point of view, his conduct was criminal.

I have heard men call for him to be hanged. Yet his conduct was natural. It was inspired by the same spirit that has kept a thousand of his kind voyaging those dangerous seas; the same spirit that had brought him and many another like him off best in U-boat duels; the same spirit that animated that fine old skipper of the North Seas who, with both legs shot off and his vessel sinking, ordered his crew to throw him and the code books into the sea together. So let us accept his repentance, and permit the incident, unfortunately one of many, serve to illustrate at once the merits and faults of the convoy system.

CHAPTER 17

The Convoy System

The merits of the convoy system, taking them first, have been abundantly proved by the decrease in mercantile sinking since the old patrol system was abandoned. Under the latter the destroyer and patrol fleets were scattered like pawns over a vast checkerboard that ruled off British waters, and across which merchant vessels moved from one check to another. Though they were hunted incessantly, the U-boats managed to pick up in those days somewhere between thirty and fifty ships a week. But, after Allied shipping was grouped in convoys and sent through the danger zone under destroyer escorts, the weekly average fell to eighteen large ships or less and four or five small ones. During the last eight months of 1917, indeed, the American and British destroyer fleets convoyed over one hundred and fifty thousand vessels in and out of Allied ports, with a loss of one eighth of one per cent.

Perhaps the best proof of the effectiveness of the convoy system is furnished by the English Channel passage. Through the lanes of destroyers, aeroplanes, "blimps," transports, and supply-ships have moved for three years with perfect safety. Now an ocean-going convoy is merely a section of Channel passage far out at sea, and, if as well guarded, is equally safe.

A certain number of destroyers to a certain number of merchant vessels has been required for perfect safety, and that convoys of thirty vessels with a quarter their number of destroyers are practically safe was proved, at least to my satisfaction, on a cruise I recently made when a number of our vessels escorted a total of sixty vessels a distance of eighteen hundred miles in ten days through waters infested with submarines.

To the right and left, ahead and astern, U-boats were constantly being reported. Often we crossed their courses. No doubt they had us under observation most of the time. But—mark this—we sank the only one that had the nerve to attack us, and sent its crew of four officers and thirty men back to our base. Another significant fact: while we passed in safety, unescorted vessels were being sunk all around us. Five were torpedoed, indeed, in less than four hours; three of which went to the bottom.

As a matter of fact, the bulk of the U-boat weekly bag is taken from the unescorted ships. A further advantage is to be found in the fact that, no matter how much the German may increase the number of his submarines, whether an attack be delivered by one or more U-boats, a properly escorted convoy is reasonably safe.

If this be true, the question naturally arises—why are merchant ships ever allowed to go out alone? The answer is simple: we have not destroyers enough to go around. Were it otherwise, the submarine war would be over.

In the meantime, till we get enough, the American and British naval authorities are doing the best they can. By the use of small patrol-boats, "blimps," and hydroplanes, they manage to keep large areas of home waters safe for local traffic, and to keep certain sea lanes open through which fast merchant vessels can escape to the high seas beyond the danger zone.

Once in a while the U-boats break into these protected areas, however, and, though they find it a costly business that usually ends in their extermination, the weekly record of mercantile sinkings still may take a jump.

Another reason why vessels are permitted to go out alone touches the convoy system's chief disadvantage: it reduces tonnage, or carrying capacity, first, by delays waiting for escorts; second, by limiting the speed of fast ships.

The ship on which I went from New York to Liverpool, for instance, is a seven days' boat. Two others in our convoy were equally fast. Yet, by being forced to take speed of the slowest vessel, we took sixteen days to cross, time enough for the three vessels to have got back to New York. In other words, less material can be moved under the convoy system than by free ships.

Nevertheless, we cannot get on without it. It is wholly impossible to maintain safe codes with merchant shipping scattered all over the world. To control its routing and divert it in accordance with enemy movements, it is absolutely essential to group it under war vessels.

The great reduction, almost half, in sunken mercantile tonnage since the adoption of the system also far more than makes up for delays and lost speed.

CHAPTER 18

U-Boat Limitations

The limitations and advantages of convoys being thus understood, let us consider for a moment those of the U-boats. Instead of being as free as the fish, they are compelled to operate within quite narrow lines, while exposed to many risks that do not menace surface craft. Think of the uncharted rocks, tips of underseas mountains, that must project up into the deep lanes along which the U-boat blunders like a blind fish; the minefields, both British and German, it must avoid; floating mines that have broken from their moorings; the treacherous tides, traps, decoys, nets, that make of a U-boat journey one long, blind hazard.

To these special risks have to be added the usual sea dangers, storms, fogs, contrary winds and tides. I have heard of one U-boat that strayed into the famous maelstrom, the giant whirlpool that was selected by Jules Verne to kill off Captain Nemo and his *Nautilus*, the terror of the seas, forty years ago. Then think of the war risks—the "blimps," hydroplanes dropping their bombs from the sky; the little patrol-boats always ready to engage in one of those desperate sea duels where no quarter is asked or given; and, finally, the destroyer, which because of its swiftness and agility remains the U-boat's chief foe. So deadly a foe is the destroyer, indeed, that the Germans have talked both loudly and long of underseas cruisers to chase it off the seas.

By certain alarmists among us this boasting was given credence—just as the German intended. Most of it was manufactured, as a matter of fact, for foreign consumption. The Hun naval authorities are quite aware of certain limitations that make against such a boat. Add armour-plate to a vessel and her size must be increased to provide more buoyancy. Increased bulk calls for heavier internal structure, heavier engines, heavier gun platforms for larger guns, larger quarters for a larger crew, larger fuel and water ballast tanks: all of which calls for more buoyancy, that is, increased size, which once more demands more armour, and so on.

Such a vessel, if produced, would present a deeper target for a torpedo than any destroyer, and only one would be required to send her to the bottom. She would stand a poor chance in a standup battle with the group of destroyers that are always to be found with a convoy. She would also require a full hundred feet of water for safe manoeuvring, and would so find it quite difficult to operate among the shoals and shallows of British home waters, where her prey would be principally found.

Lastly, she could give chase to only one vessel at a time, so on the whole would be less effective than the present type of U-boats. As two years have passed since the Germans first talked of "underseas cruisers," we can rest assured that, after balancing the increased cost in time, labour,, money and materials against possible advantages, the German naval constructors have pronounced against them. There is no good reason for us to make a nightmare out of this particular German dream.

There are also decided limitations in submarine navigation and operations. The popular idea of a U-boat emerging and diving again with porpoise ease is quite erroneous. Abrupt dives are very dangerous. A submarine commander told me that his hair had often stood on end when, on a quick dive, his vessel went down and down till he thought he could never stop her. Doubtless many a U-boat has gone headlong into the deep where the terrific pressure would crush her iron sides like an eggshell. Once on the surface, a large U-boat would require several minutes to submerge, and if she be seen by a destroyer, her fate is almost surely sealed; for, no matter to what depth she may go, the telltale wake floats up to the surface. A depth-mine barrage closes the incident.

Neither can a U-boat cruise indefinitely under water. Seventy to a hundred miles is the limit. After that it must come up to recharge its batteries while steaming along the surface. If it be sighted on emerging with its batteries exhausted, its situation becomes desperate. There is a case on record of three German submarines so caught, which lay for forty-eight hours on the bottom, listening to the *chug, chug* of the patrol screws above. Two that tried to sneak away in the night were sunk. The third surrendered.

Surface cruising also has its limits. At low speeds a submarine's

SUBMARINE CHASERS IN VARIOUS STAGES OF CONSTRUCTION

SUBMARINE CHASERS AWAITING TRANSPORTATION TO THE OTHER SIDE

radius runs up to six or seven thousand miles, but a good deal of this mileage is used up in coming and going between the hunting-grounds and the base, and if much high speed work is done in long stern chases after fleeing merchant vessels, the mileage is further cut down. On the average, a U-boat can stay away from its base between twenty and twenty-five days.

To extend this time limit, many attempts have been made to establish supply bases in the hunting waters. Food can be obtained, of course, from captured ships, but fuel comes less easily. One ingenious commander used to *cache* barrels of fuel oil and petrol, loot from tankers, at the bottom of the sea in a sheltered cove. But one day an insignificant marker buoy in the middle of an "oil spot" betrayed him. The customary procedure would have been to carry off the barrels; but, with a flash of genius, the British commander removed the bungs, poured a few gallons of picric acid, a powerful explosive, into each barrel, then sunk them again. In racing automobiles a few drops of picric acid is sometimes added to the petrol to give it a "kick"; but it has to be done very carefully or the engine is liable to be wrecked; so it does not require much imagination to picture the fate of that particular U-boat.

Neither does the U-boat have things all its own way in the duels with merchant vessels. It fights, indeed, at a disadvantage. For, whereas a score of shells may fail to put a fleeing ship out of commission, one well planted shot will send a submarine to the bottom; and there is always the danger of the pursued turning like a wounded bull and charging over the pursuer. Again, though German torpedoes have a range of six or seven thousand yards, shooting is very uncertain at such distances. A U-boat usually tries to get within one thousand yards of its prey. This, especially in shots at a convoy, entails greater danger, for the U-boat's position can easily be gaged by the torpedo's wake. A depth-mine barrage, again, is almost certain to do the business.

Then rough weather brings a pause in the hunting. Rising high above the deck, the periscope describes a far wider arc than the hull, which threshes around like a wounded whale, making both observation and the sighting of shots impossible. In such weather, the U-boats run for a sheltered shore with a sandy bottom and lie there till the storm blows over. During the extremely bad weather in November, 1917, the U-boat bag fell from twenty-four ships to six in the first week.

All of the dangers and difficulties above set forth are intensified by accurate reports of U-boat movements from observation stations on land and ships at sea, and while cruising with our fleet I was astonished by the number that streamed in to our bridge every day. Position and course were usually given; so, besides drawing the patrols after them, the reports cause all merchant-ships to avoid that particular vicinity. They quite accounted for the despairing note in a radio we picked up, one evening, in transit between two U-boats.

Have you seen any ships today? The ocean seems to be empty.

This commander, no doubt, was one of those whose pessimistic reports caused the German government to account for the decrease in the weekly bag in the following grandiloquent terms:

Enemy shipping has been so depleted by the attacks of our in-vincible U-boats that it is becoming very difficult to find ships to sink.

This in a week that had seen forty-six hundred ships sail in and out of British ports alone, and probably half as many more from the harbours of Allied nations.

Summing the U-boat's potentialities, we find that it is limited in cruising radius and operations; is exposed to extra sea and war risks; is, in fact, a hunted creature—hunted, moreover, so successfully that the British First Lord was able to report in Parliament:

We are sinking forty or fifty *per cent*, of German submarines.

The loss of the vessels, it should be remembered, is aggravated by that of the torpedoes they carry. The small boats usually carry two, the large and later types about twenty.

Now, a torpedo is an extremely complex piece of mechanism that takes months of time and thousands of dollars to build. Indeed, the en-tire yearly output of the United States naval torpedo works, before the war, was only twelve. Accordingly, if a U-boat is sunk outward bound with a full complement of twenty torpedoes—which happens quite often—their loss is more serious than that of the vessel. It is highly improbable that any U-boat goes down without some torpedoes. It is also comforting to know that an average of four or five torpedoes are shot away for every vessel sunk. The twenty vessels sunk each week costs the German government in torpedoes alone close to half a mil-lion dollars.

Such a mortality in crews, torpedoes, and submarines could only be justified by a far greater accomplishment than has been so far achieved. The life of a U-boat commander has never been considered a good insurance risk. In 1017, he made two voyages and a half before, quite literally, he went down and out. From present indications it would seem that in 1918 his life will not be worth the toss of a coin.

For in the underseas war the German has lost. His threat to *bring England to her knees*—and by England he meant the whole world—was writ on the wide waters, scratched on the sea-sands. The tide of events has washed it away. In the attempt to fulfil it he piled cruelty upon cruelty, frightfulness upon frightfulness; but they reacted upon himself. Like the dragon's teeth in the classic myth, the cruelties he sowed broadcast on land and water sprang up against him in new crops of armed men. His infernal labours have brought him naught but loathing and contempt of a proscribed race, his sentence is already to be read upon the wall, for in his gamble with the Fates, he staked all on one last desperate throw on the U-boat. Losing that, he loses all.

CHAPTER 19

"Damn the Torpedoes! Steam Right Ahead!"

When Farragut shouted his famous order from the shrouds of his ship at Mobile, he could not foresee that he was establishing a precedent which, fifty years later, was to become the ordinary every-day watchword of another American fleet.

Between the "torpedoes" of Farragut's time and those which our destroyers in European waters are called upon to dodge each day, there is, however, a great difference. His were merely mines—clumsy affairs at that, altogether lacking the tremendous explosive force of those which the German submarines spew out as a cod lays eggs in Allied waters. In addition to this devil's bread which he thus casts upon the waters it is comforting to know that it sometimes "returns to him after many days," for more than one German submarine has nosed off its own mines—Fritz always keeps a couple of torpedoes gaged at a depth of six feet for the especial benefit of Yankee destroyers.

He shoots them, too, at every safe chance; for, in spite of his "will to conquer," Fritz is an earnest believer in the doctrine of "safety first." Though for the last nine months he has taken pot shots at our destroyers time and again, so far he has scored few hits. The last, I am sorry to say, was a bull's-eye—the sorrier because I had cruised for two weeks in company with the *Jacob Jones*, and knew some of her officers and crew.

Previous to her sinking, the *Cassin*, another of our destroyers, had had her stern blown off; and, though up to the time this single casualty was all that had been scored against our fleet during an eight months' campaign in mined waters against an unseen foe, it was made the text of a bitter editorial in an American paper. Sitting, without doubt, in a comfortable office, unaware of the hardships and real suffering the men he was attacking endure, with a lack of sympathy that is equalled only by his blind ignorance, this omnipotent gentleman wrote:

THE NAVY FALLS DOWN

Outside the sorrow and anger that will sweep America at the direct hit registered by a German submarine against one of our boasted destroyers and the outright sinking of a convoyed transport (the *Antilles*), the news of the two reverses to our naval efficiency in warring waters cannot but be wholesome in its ultimate effect. . . . The torpedoing of a destroyer, the craft so fast, so agile and alert that they have been considered the one thing afloat that may, with proper alertness, laugh at the lumbersome submarine and its leisurely torpedo speed, reflects on no one but the officers and crew of the torpedoed destroyers. These humiliating hits by the Germans are directly chargeable to their inefficiency and carelessness.

The article contains a good deal of this silly and untruthful nonsense. The *Antilles*, in the first instance, was not convoyed by a destroyer, but by one of those armed yachts that are serving in French waters under a handicap of low speed. In the second place, the hit registered on the *Cassin*, and the sinking of the *Jacob Jones*, are ordinary chances of war. Moreover, we have been exceedingly fortunate to escape so lightly. In the eight months preceding the first casualty our flotilla had steamed jointly over a million miles, a distance equivalent to the circling of the world forty times—steamed it in mined seas, subject at all times to the attacks of submarines. The British destroyer officers wondered at our luck. Luck! it was luck—also fine seamanship.

Compare this record with the hard experience of the British, who handed over to us the sea lore learned during the three years of war at the cost of many disasters. Think of the swift cruisers, battleships, great dreadnoughts that lie with their fine crews, thousands in number, at the bottom of the sea! Scarcely a family in Great Britain that is not mourning some drowned sailor lad.

Think of the trawlers and little patrol-boats that sail forth with all of the swank of a dreadnought to hunt the elusive submarine! Scores of them never return. Others come limping back into port with little left but a hull and screw. One I saw that had been torpedoed astern had her propeller-shaft bent up and over until the screw looked into the engine hatch, and she looked for all the world like a happy dog wagging its tail.

What of the mine-sweepers and their hard-bit crews that wrest dangerous weapons from the very hands of death?

What of the Q-boats which go out looking for things from which even a destroyer will run! One of their skippers wears the Victoria Cross with the bar of a second achievement; also every other decoration it is possible for a fighting mariner to win. He has been blown up so often that it has become something of a bore—never a thrill left in it. His ship has been sunk under him three times, and on the last occasion he served his guns till the water rose to the breasts of the crew, and sank the attacking submarine with the last shot before the deck went from under their feet.

Apart from their losses in battle, which have been large, the British destroyer flotilla loses on an average one vessel a month. So no wonder they marvel at our luck. They, however, do not squeal. When two of their destroyers were towed into port, one with its bows shot away, the other without a stern, they did not waste time writing editorials on the inefficiency of the officers and crews. The British are not built that way. They just took these two vessels and sawed their ends off clean; then, just as you might solder a tin toy boat, they joined the two odd halves to make one, and sent the result out to sea. And this little feat symbolizes their spirit—the dogged, quiet, uncomplaining devotion to duty which they share with our own American officers and men.

Having seen the *Cassin* just after she was torpedoed, and talked with members of her crew, and having cruised, as I said before, in company with the *Jacob Jones*, I can claim to be in better position to pass judgment than the author of the editorial quoted, and the facts are these:

Let us take the last first, and recreate as well as we can the picture of what actually happened from the reports of her commander and crew. She and other destroyers were returning to their base after delivering a convoy at a foreign port; but as she had paused to carry out target practice at sea, the others were out of sight ahead.

Imagine her, that graceful boat, careening as she swung on the turns of her zigzag course at standard speed, officers on the bridge, watches set, crew in their berths below or smoking on deck, all things following their orderly bent. At 4:30 p. m. dusk was already falling in those winter seas. It would be impossible to see the finger periscope that was probably slipped up just long enough to sight the shot. First notice came when the officer on the bridge saw the torpedo coming at the editor's "leisurely speed" of forty-two miles an hour.

He did the right thing—jammed the helm "hard left" and rang the engine-room for "emergency high speed." As the boat leaped under the sudden hard thrust of the screws and began to swing like a scared thing, he could see the red warhead of the torpedo as it "porpoised" along the surface, leaping from wave to wave. Once it lifted clean out of the water and swerved, and he thought it might pass astern. But the instant it dived again the deviation automatically corrected. It struck a trifle aft of amidships, and exploded in the fuel oil tank.

The explosion blew twenty feet of the deck clean away, brought down the wireless mast and antennae—leaving the vessel dumb, unable to call her consorts ahead—flooded the after crew quarters and steaming fire-room, from which not one man escaped alive.

So terrific was the explosion the starboard torpedo tube with its two torpedoes, weighing many tons, was blown 200 feet in midair. Yet this was only the beginning. Poised astern, ready to drop on a submarine, were two depth-mines charged with TNT. Two other mines were lashed close by to the deck. One of these "careless and inefficient" officers ran back, at the risk of his life, to try and set the explosion gear of the mines at "safe." But the stern sank before he could reach them.

Eight minutes after the torpedo struck she sank. But in that eight minutes—listen to what was done. But first picture the scene: imagine the debris flying high in the air, the crash of falling masts, the stupefying roar of successive explosions; the men lying dead and dying about the decks, some floating in the water; the pall of smoke and escaping steam! Now what was done?

The gun crews stood to their guns in readiness for a shot at the submarine. An auxiliary engine was rigged on to the lighting system and a wireless improvised in a vain effort to send out a low-power S.O.S. The life-rafts were launched—the boats, alas, were smashed. The splinter mats that protect the bridge from shrapnel fire, huge mattresses five feet square, were cut away and thrown overboard with the life-buoys to hold up struggling swimmers.

The effort to rig up a wireless failing for lack of time, the guns were repeatedly fired to attract attention. When she began to sink her bows rose almost perpendicular while she twisted a half circle. But just before that happened the commander had run along the deck, ordering everybody into the water. As she sank he stepped off himself into the sea.

While there, swimming for his life, shaken by the loss of his ship, stupefied by the tremendous concussions, and surrounded by his dead and drowning men, the habit of discipline was still so strong, his spirit so fine, that he took accurate note of the submarine when she popped up out of the water. Listen to this—from a man who could see at that moment nothing but slow drowning ahead:

> The submarine approached within six hundred yards, picked up one survivor, then submerged again. It appeared to be between one hundred and fifty and two hundred and fifty feet long. It carried a three-inch gun forward of the conning-tower, and the periscopes were housed. Her general appearance was that of the U-51-56 class, but her conning-tower was like those of the U-49 class.

He says of his officers and men that "they were cool, calm, and helpful to each other," and the sequel proved it. Though greatly weakened by cold and exposure, one officer swam from one raft to another in an endeavour to equalize their weights. He died, poor fellow, in the night from cold and exposure; but the survivors all say of him: "He was game to the end."

A boatswain's mate stripped off his own clothing to try and warm his dying officer.

At the risk of almost certain death, one fine lad had stayed in the motor sailor boat till the ship sank, trying to cast loose the lashings and get it off. If he had succeeded twenty more lives would have been saved; but his failure in no way dims the shining courage of his act.

The death record contains again and again the entry opposite a name, "Died from cold and exposure and was dropped overboard to lighten the raft." So, even in death, the poor fellows aided the living by easing them higher above the waves.

Two officers and sixty-four men gave up their lives that night, but they did not die in vain. They had played their part in protecting thousands of supply-ships. They helped to feed the starving millions of Europe; to carry on the war against the Hun. And they are not unavenged. They made their own settlement in full with the submarines. One of the vessel's reports on an engagement reads: "The sea was immediately covered with floating oil to the full size of the submarine, and a man's body was seen by members of the crew."

The British Admiralty is very conservative. It does not allow a "sinking" except on undisputed evidence. Now, if a mine explodes above a submarine, it sends her straight to the bottom, and all that one sees is more or less oil. Oil reports show frequently in the sunken destroyer's record, so we know that, besides those credited to her, there were doubtless others. Like a good fighter, she wreaked her own vengeance before she fell. Peace to her! Peace to the fine lads that lie with her at the bottom of the sea!

Now for the other casualty, the *Cassin*. Here again imagine the actual conditions. Two inches of periscope, no larger than a floating beer-bottle, suddenly emerges from a choppy sea half a mile away. An eagle's vision could not find it. As in the other case, first warning comes from the torpedo, the lightning stroke of death, racing across the sea. There's a yell from the lookout; the clang of the engine-room bell. The vessel swings on her heels—too late. The torpedo strikes astern in the after crew's quarters.

Fourteen men were down in that compartment, which was practically blown away. One man's feet were touching a frame that was fused by the intense heat engendered by the explosion. Looking at the mass of twisted wreckage later, I could hardly believe it possible that any person could have come out of that compartment alive. Yet, with the exception of a fractured ankle suffered by the one man, they all escaped unhurt.

Why? Because of one man's sacrifice. On watch aft, he saw the torpedo heading straight for the stern, where two depth-mines hung ready for use. He knew the compartment was full of men. He had seen a depth-mine raise a column of water thirty-five yards wide a hundred feet above the sea. He knew what they could do. It would have been quite easy for him to run forward to safety, but that sense of duty, which rises in our race superior to the fear of death, dominated the lad. Like the officer on the other sunken ship, he ran aft in a desperate race with the torpedo to reach and set the mines at "safe." His hands were on them when the torpedo struck. He went up with them in the air; but that he had made them safe is proved by the fact that they did not explode till high above the deck.

If this lad had been in the British Navy, his wife, mother, sister or other surviving relative would have received the Victoria Cross that his courage and sacrifice had earned. We have no such decoration. In place thereof our editor, sitting in his warm office with his feet on a carpeted floor, uses the incident as a peg on which to hang his statement that "The Navy Falls Down." Save the mark!

Common justice calls for the statement that the *Cassin* could not have been more skilfully handled. With all her stern blown off above the propeller, one screw and her rudder gone, she kept going. She could only steam in slow circles. But, circling thus, like a wounded hawk, she turned such a hot fire on the submarine, when it came up to deliver a finishing blow, that it dived again and scooted like a scared crab from the dangerous vicinity.

Great seamanship was shown in getting the ship back to port, but it is a tale too long for my space. Sufficient that, combined with the gallantry displayed by the officers and crews of both vessels, the courage, fortitude and seaman-ship displayed by all, these casualties are raised to the ranks of achievements worthy to go down in the history of our Navy.

Surely we must expect casualties. Our officers and crews do. As one sailor lad put it: "We never know when we'll kick over a mine."

On the occasion that I went out with part of the fleet, we manoeuvred for two hours in waters that we found out afterward had just been mined by a submarine. All in the day's work—and taken as such by the fellows who do it. And if they are willing to accept the risk, they to whom a torpedoing or the "kicking over a mine" means death, surely we landlubbers, who live at home at ease, ought to try and emulate their spirit.

The ever-present danger is, however, the least of the destroyer sailor's troubles. He thinks more of the incessant hardships to which he is exposed. The vessels go out and stay out in all weathers, and let me tell you from experience that there is nothing in the way of motion on earth at once so insidiously sickening and yet so violent as that of a destroyer in a heavy sea.

A son of mine happens to be on a United States destroyer, and this is the description he gives of a recent storm:

> We were caught in a howling gale—the worst storm I ever saw in the eight years I have been to sea. The wind blew with a velocity of a hundred and ten miles an hour. The ocean was one huge, mountainous sea. Our decks were swept clean of all movable objects, tool-chests, boats and so forth. All of the living compartments were flooded with water; everything was wet; and, to make it worse, the thermometer dropped away below freezing point. For thirty-six hours we lay hove to, riding it out, before we could go about our duty.

"Some weather!" Before the war it would have been considered impossible for a destroyer to live through it. A commander who sent out a ship in a gale like that might have been court-martialed for imperil-ling the lives of his officers and men. But now they go out and stay out as a matter of course, never even thinking of trying to come in.

Though less uncomfortable, the fogs that drop a thick gray blanket over the seas are far more wearing on the nerves. Imagine half a dozen destroyers guarding a thirty-vessel convoy. At night a fog-bank closes around them before they can scatter, and from an exact science navi-gation degenerates into the blind groping of a blind navigator over blind seas. Not a commander in our fleet but has collected an assort-ment of nightmares in such weather to last him the rest of his life. Not a sailor that cannot relate hair-raising experiences such as these:

Out of the thick pea-soup fog a huge black freighter suddenly rose on our bows. As we swung on our heel with one screw reversed, a destroyer came shooting at us from the opposite quarter. Avoiding her, we almost ran down another steamer. I tell you, for a while gray hell was loose there on a black sea.

They have not always escaped. Fogs have caused many casualties. Few of our destroyers have gone through the year without acquiring smashed bows or bent plates. The *Chauncey*, rammed and sunk with all her officers in the Mediterranean, has, so far, been the one fatality. But we cannot always expect such luck, so let us spend no further time in foolish criticism.

Our sailors go forth every day to face fogs and storms in mined seas. Theirs the hardships and dangers; ours the loyal, unswerving sup-port. In order to do their best, they must know that the home folks stand behind them.

CHAPTER 20

The Hun "Harriers"

I got my first glimpse of the "harriers" from a high hill at the harbour mouth as they came in from a U-boat hunt.

From that height their small oval decks appeared to be pinned flat on the green baize of the sea, and as they approached in long lines, a feather of white wake behind each boat, they looked exactly what they were—one of those wide-toothed combs that drag English waters day and night for the U-boat, that most pestiferous of ocean's creatures. Their precise movement, the accuracy of the zigzags which laid the diagonal crossed lace of their wakes in diagonal patterns on the pale jade of the sea, made a fine spectacle in the vast amphitheatre of sky and ocean. Not till they turned into file and passed around the end of the long break-water, did I walk downhill to the base, where I found them huddling like tired hounds under the stone quay wall.

It is our habit to invest the inanimate with our own personal feelings, but in their case "tired" was no exaggeration. After days of heavy buffeting by Channel seas, their engines were foul, and needed rest, adjustment, and a clean-up, just as much as their greasy, sea-worn crews. By contrast, the boats that were going out to take their places looked like blooded hounds straining on the leash. I was slated to go with them; and, having found the—let us call her the *Noughty-nine* , I climbed from the high stone dock down to her deck.

Just now she was in the throes of the "get-away"—stores being stowed; depth-mines hoisted into position; guns shotted; motors clattering in the engine-room. It was all very grim and warlike—not a whit less so because every man on board had been following the pursuits of peace less than a year ago. The fact, indeed, linked them with Raleigh, Drake, Frobisher, Hawkins, those stout old freebooters of the time of "good Queen Bess" who put to sea with green crews from this very dock, hundreds of years ago, to ravage the Spanish Main and carry on where Columbus left off. Undoubtedly those were days of great adventure in a half-known world; yet, as I looked over the *Noughty-nine* and noted her "bridge," no larger than the conning-tower of a submarine, the tiny deck, and general miniature proportions, I could not but think that the voyage of this cockle-shell fleet across the Atlantic was worthy of its time.

The story of it, indeed, reads like a minor *Odyssey*. Designed to carry a certain weight, the boats were all loaded, starting out, with extra stores and gadgets; and when a big storm blew up a few days later, "Headquarters" was rather anxious for their safety. It hung breathlessly, so to speak, on the wireless that was recording their struggle against mountainous seas in mid-Atlantic.

For a week their navigation was almost submarine, for the seas washed continuously over the wheelhouse; to look out was like peering through a submerged periscope. All that time the crews ate dry food, hard-tack, corned beef, and the like, helped out by an occasional cup of coffee. They could neither shave, wash, nor sleep for the violent motion. "Headquarters" pinned its faith on their two tenders, powerful tugs that were mothering the fleet across. In case anything happened, they would be there to stand by. But when the final report came in—the tugs had foundered.

And they had other adventures. At a distance, a chaser's upper works strongly resemble those of a submarine. Consequently they share, to a certain extent, the hectic existence of those Ishmaelites of the sea, the American and English submarines that are hunting the U-boats through Allied waters. At night or in hazy weather every man's hand is against them. They may be shot at with impartiality by destroyers, patrols, and merchantmen. The last named, however, have a decided preference for ramming. Almost all the chasers have had experiences similar to the one related by the second officer, who joined me in the wheel-house after we were under way:

The weather was a bit thick when, at dusk, a big black hull suddenly hove up dead on our beam. A belch of smoke and sparks from her funnels told that she had seen us and thrown into the high, and as she came charging down on us like a mad elephant, we could see her three masts in line against the sky. I tell you, she looked wicked and big—big as a runaway mountain. Even after we fired signals, she kept on coming, her masts still in line.

Not till she was almost on top of us did she begin to veer, and even then she passed so close that I could have spat on her side as she passed.

Quite an experience for a man who, till a year ago, had no more knowledge of the sea than can be learned in the mountains and deserts of Colorado. Yet, looking at him, alert, capable, conning the *Noughty-nine* and issuing his orders with the authority and decision of a seasoned salt, one could not but wonder at the magic that has transformed thousands of landsmen in the chaser service into capable officers and efficient crews. It would be unbelievable if they were not there in the flesh to prove it. Nor could the "blue-water navy" exhibit a finer spirit than is displayed by the "chasers," from their commander-in-chief at the base down to his coloured cook. Indeed, the answer made by the latter to a question of mine excellently represents the spirit of all:

No, boss; Ah really doan' regret coming ovah heah. 'Tain't like home, of course, but they jes' couldn't pull me back till we've finished this business right. Ah wouldn't have it said that Ah hadn't been in it for all the money in the world.

An equally proper pride showed in the answer the second officer now made to a question:

A fellow naturally favours his own service, but when it comes to a question of hard work and results, we chasers think we have it on the destroyers. A score of chasers, in the first place, can be built for the cost of one destroyer; and, as we are equipped with the guns, depth-mines, wireless, and hydrophones they carry, we are every bit as efficient in an offensive.

All the destroyer has on us is speed; but it would take a mighty lively bird to cover the patrols that can be cared for by a brace of chasers. For convoy work, of course, where high speed and long cruises are called for, we can't compete. But we can carry on almost as long, and stay out in worse weather, for just when a blow begins to bother them it ceases to trouble us. You ought to have been out with us in the last big storm. She rode the waves like a trim duck. Up we'd go quartering across an enormous swell almost to the crest, but not quite make it and go side-slipping down into the deep trough. It was an awfully queer sensation.

He went on, grinning:

At home they named us the 'Slackers' Paradise' from the initials of 'Submarine Patrol'—I suppose because some of the fellows lived at home and came down to the boat every morning. But I'd like to have had some of those snap-shot nicknamers out on patrol in the snow and sleet and ice off the Maine coast. As for over here,—(he nodded at the barometer, which was falling fast)—looks like you were about to have an opportunity to judge for yourself.

He said it! For, just one hour later, the smooth green mirror I had looked down on from the hill was smashed into smithereens by a nasty wind that quickly raised the waves to the exact proportions required for a chaser's worst motion. Fortunately, I had already toured the boat—otherwise it would never have been done—from the dinky fo'castle, where I found half of the crew stowed in shelf bunks very like but much smaller than the niches of a tomb; through the listening-room, where the watch sits at the hydrophones, eternally listening, listening for U-boats; into the tiny ward-room under the wheel-house, about six feet by eight, jammed with a desk, chair, typewriter, arms, instruments, clothing, and books on navigation; finally the mess-room, a small box about five feet square, where four men can sit at a swing table within arm's reach of the cook's stove at the other side of a thin partition. Till that functionary opened the door and let in a gush of frying odours along with the pork chop he thrust without fair warning under my nose, I had scarcely noticed the motion. But after that? Well, as I moved forward from the rail to the wheel-house half an hour later, a sadder and emptier man, the commander threw me a grain of comfort:

Five of the crew beat you to it.

While salving my pride, the knowledge did not ease my qualms. It would be easy to describe a night of horrors, to picture the little vessel staggering like a drunken juggler over enormous black night seas, now rearing up on its screws, again standing on its bows. To tell the truth, much cruising on destroyers had accustomed me to seasickness, so that I did not mind it much. Lying in the commander's bunk, I absorbed between—er, spasms—chaser lore as it issued from a mausoleum niche occupied by the second officer opposite. On my inner side a row of navigation books persistently tried to edge me out—and

SUBMARINE CHASERS STARTING OUT ON SPEED TEST

SUBMARINE CHASERS ON PRELIMINARY SPEED TEST

succeeded once, when a particularly heavy roll put me out on the floor and distributed them over me in a learned shower. Leaving them there, I crawled back in, and presently obtained a new experience when a great voice, raised almost to a bellow by an amplifying device, roared at us by wireless telephony from another chaser a mile away.

"Why did you turn on your running lights?" it inquired with insulting violence; and rejected with explosive force our modest suggestion that we had merely followed its owner's example. Just who got the best of the argument I cannot say, for it was cut off by an "Allo" that gave the position of a U-boat—unfortunately, too far away to be of any use to us. Nevertheless, it served a good purpose in stimulating the second officer—who had fallen into a doze—to a renewal of conversation.

> That fellow is cruising dangerously close to a minefield. I beg the Admiralty's pardon, (he corrected, laughing)—I mean a prohibited area. However, under any old name that Hun bird will find it just as dangerous.
> I had a talk the other day, by the way, with a Limey officer concerning the etiquette to be observed in case you happen to chase a U-boat into a mine—I mean, prohibited area. To depth-bomb him or not to? that was the question
> 'If you do,' he replied, 'you will undoubtedly blow yourself up and possibly touch off the whole area. Fancy how you would look sailing up out of an explosion twenty miles square!' But he qualified: 'Of course if you got the Hun it would be worth it, and there wouldn't be a splinter left of you big enough to hold a court of inquiry on. You'd all go to glory with a bang!'

As a matter of fact, more than one U-boat has so ended its piratical career "with a bang!"—for prohibited areas carry no signs, "*Verboten!*" Any U-boat is welcome to come right in, And many others, principally mine-layers, have been hoisted by their own petards. Of one crucial instance the second officer now made note:

> A strong current carried this fellow on to a nest of eggs he had just laid at the mouth of an Allied harbour. The captain, who happened to be in the conning-tower, was blown clear as the boat went down, and swam around till picked up by a patrol-boat that investigated the explosion. He had shed his clothes in the water, and represented himself as the sole survivor of a Norwegian vessel sunk by a mine. And he almost got away with

it—not quite, however, for your Hun can always be depended upon to overplay a part. As the Limey skipper pertinently remarked, 'The fellow was too damned fluent.' So they took him down to the ward-room and gave him a few drinks to 'keep him from taking cold.' Whereupon, *in vino veritas,*—didn't the old Romans know it?—he let out the truth. Next day, while he journeyed to an internment camp, a couple of mine-sweepers swept up his boat.

A particularly vicious roll uncoffined the second officer, just then, from his niche. After he had climbed back, he went on:

Those Limey officers are a fine lot. A bit hard to get acquainted with, of course. They don't plunge into friendship in our slap-dash fashion. But after they do give themselves there's no finer brand of friendship than the article the Limeys put up. Oh, it's a neat package. And they are *so* courteous under all conditions. When the *P*—— picked up the survivors of a hospital-ship after twelve hours' exposure, they were so exhausted they had to be lifted over the side. Among them was a naval Limey, and when one of our chaps told him how glad we were to have him on board, he replied in his quiet English way, 'A pleasure, I assure you'—then fainted and lay unconscious for nine hours afterward.

In the interest of his yarns I had almost forgotten to be seasick, but after he dozed off again the little beast of a boat made up for my lapsed time. It shook and pounded and kneaded and rolled me into a wretched human paste. One second it would stand me on my head, the next set me violently upon my heels. And its lateral side-slips were simply appalling. With malice aforethought, it would simulate a lull, and just when—let us be frank—I reached for the pail, it would achieve a most remarkable combination of *jiu-jitsu* and Graeco-Turkish wrestling in a determined effort to put me to the floor.

It showed particular malice when, next morning, the steward brought me tea and dry toast. "Eat, will you?" it seemed to reflect. "We'll see." And see it did, letting loose in a paroxysm of high kicking and buck-jumping that would have shamed the best efforts of a Western "outlaw." I passed up—not literally—the tea and toast. Likewise— this time literally—a cup of soup at lunch.

Yet, though I fell in with a proposal to transfer me to the destroyer that had charge of the hunt, I would not have missed the experience, or have its discomforts wiped from my memory. For it revealed just what these chaser sailors must have endured in the big storm coming across; what they will be called upon to endure the coming winter; what they will be enduring, indeed, when these lines get into print. Next to the submarines, with whom I cruised eight days on patrol, I take off my hat to the chasers, and would extend to them the same remuneration of two hundred and sixty thousand dollars a year which, with frequent vacations, seems to me appropriate payment for their service.

Though the entire fleet had pulled into the lea of a group of islands, my transfer to the destroyer was still a ticklish job. But even this experience was valuable, for it revealed just why so many poor souls have been drowned by capsizing boats launched in bad weather from torpedoed ships. I had never fancied myself a "Jonah." So far, indeed, I had brought luck to my ships, for three previous cruises had yielded a net profit of one U-boat captured and another sunk. It had been suggested, because of this, that our government ought to subsidize me to go to sea on its ships. It may be, however, that my "joss-ship" does not extend to the weather. In any case, after the *Noughty-nine* threw me overboard, the wind immediately died, the long seas subsided. That night the destroyer dipped to a gentle ground-swell. Morning broke with golden sunshine flooding the whole world between a brilliant green sea and dappled sky.

And now the "hunt" began in earnest. Allied coastal waters are a giant chess-board on which U-boats and chasers play a blindfold game. The destroyer in the centre, chasers lining out to the horizon, we would sweep down one side of an area, then come back up the other. If an "Allo" reports a U-boat elsewhere, off goes the whole show like a pack of harriers after a hare, to reform and comb out that particular area with the anxious assiduity a mother bestows on a loved child that has consorted for a while with undesirable company. They are equally vicious with the product,—if found,—rending the very bowels of old ocean with roaring depth-mines.

Today, however, we were out of luck. Though quite near, the Hun shark gave no sign of his presence. But as, that night in the captain's cabin, I was sleeping the sound sleep of the exhausted seasick person, a voice issued from the speaking-tube at my ear, reporting a wireless from *Noughty-nine*:

"Heard a U-boat. Followed up and attacked with depth-mines. Dropped two at distance not exceeding three hundred and twenty yards. Large oil patch on surface."

Fancy having a thing like that injected into your beauty sleep! It projected in my vision a cinema of the U-boat swimming lazily like a sleepy whale in the black vaults of the sea. Followed an interior such as I had had under my eyes for eight days and nights on my submarine cruise—the Hun watch sitting silently before their clocks and dials; the officer writing up his log, or lost in that thoughtful musing which is one half of submarine life; the darkness and silence of the sleeping-chambers beyond the central operating room. A booming, rending explosion! Crashing of rent plates, smashed machinery! Darkness wrapping the descent of the U-boat in a whorl of black water to the ocean floor. Which vivid imaginings were rudely dissipated by the captain's comment at breakfast next morning:

"I doubt whether they got him."

Scepticism that was justified when, later, an "Allo" came in from a seaplane thirty miles away: "Have just dropped a bomb on U-boat. "

It was undoubtedly our wounded fish, bombed again as it emerged, *in extremis*, gasping for breath. For your submarine is not really a fish. It belongs rather to the tribe of seals, whales, and other sea *Mammalia*. Though the longest-winded of all, it must come up in its season to fill its steel lungs with fresh air.

The news sent an electric impulse through our fleet. There broke out a veritable spasm of wig-wagging. Before it had completely subsided, there came winging out from the land four sea-planes, followed in equally swift but more ponderous flight by a dirigible balloon. And with their advent there opened before my gaze at once all of the means by which the Hun has been driven from shore waters that teem with ships out to his present almost deserted hunting grounds hundreds of miles out in the ocean. Destroyer leaping like a swift hound ahead, chasers yelping eagerly at its heels, those great fish-hawks the seaplanes circling overhead, dirigible shooting like an elongated silver comet at the horizon, it was a real hue and cry—yoicks! tally-ho! We raced over the sea in full cry after the Hun fox.

About the time we settled into our stride, the dirigible came shooting back, swung around, then keeping poised above wigwagged a message:

My orders have blown overboard. What are the signals?

Her commander was taking no chances of either being bluffed by a Hun or of sinking an Allied submarine.

Two of his crew had climbed out, and were standing on a narrow ledge on the car, which was swinging and pitching on a wide arc. No doubt their weight was keeping her to the wind, and it was quite interesting to see—to those who like a shudder in their entertainment. Personally, I don't care for it. Nevertheless, the sight of those two human atoms, swinging perilously up there three hundred feet above the sea, drove in deeper an already strong impression that we have no slackers in the Allied naval services. Battleships, destroyers, armed yachts, submarines, seaplanes, dirigibles, are all working like dogs and playing the dangerous underseas war game to the limit—more power to them!

Having gained the necessary information, the dirigible proceeded west at top speed, following up an oil streak that might have a U-boat at its head. For miles we could see it running in both directions across our bows, and, after detaching a couple of chasers to assist the "blimp," we raced on toward the square where the seaplane had bombed the Hun.

I wish I could record the bringing home of the "brush." That eager chase deserved the palms of victory. Alas! in the very heat of it, a wireless came like a blast from the huntsman's horn, calling the destroyer off to some other service. Oh, but it was hard! But naval law is like unto that of the Medes and Persians, which altereth not. Albeit not cheerfully, with many curious glances backward at the harrier pack still charging on over the horizon, we headed for the base at twenty-five knots.

Night was falling before we drew into harbour, so that stern view of the yelping pack was destined to be my last—a happy one, however, revealing them at the zenith of their activities. Did they get that Hun? *Quien sabe?* If you want credit for a sinking from the Admiralty, you must produce the goods. The answer returned to me by a grave-faced ensign at "Headquarters" two days later was very conservative: "U-boat probably damaged."

CHAPTER 21

Flying Sailors

"Who in the world are these fellows?" On the transport that brought us across, the above question was asked whenever two young fellows, whose khaki suits had the blue and gold shoulder straps of a naval lieutenant, appeared on the deck. The explanation that they belonged to the United States Naval Aviation Service, moreover, invariably produced the following exclamation:

"I didn't know we had one."

I confess to sharing the general ignorance, and when an opportunity opened for me to visit certain of our stations in France, I jumped at the chance to remedy it.

War, like poverty, makes strange bed-fellows, and I found my first station in a little coast town surrounded by peaked stone houses gray with age, and menaced by fat-bellied windmills that shook long wooden arms at it from the distance. Than the contrast between our loose-trousered sailor lads and the wooden-shoed French peasants, there could be nothing more violent. But the American sailor is a born mixer. The lads at the station get along fine with the peasants—especially the girls.

In her quaint, loose cap and high-waisted skirt, there is nothing that looks more demure than a little Breton girl, but she is not in the least averse to a flirtation. Evenings and Sundays they are to be seen, each with a sailor *beau*, strolling through the narrow streets and quaint courts, the girl talking voluble French, the boy answering in English, both perfectly happy and quite in accord.

One lad achieved the impossible when he wooed, won, and married the prettiest girl of the lot without being able to speak a word of French. They call it, at the station, "the marriage by dictionary." From the confession of both deponents, it appears to have been a case of love at first sight—the head-over-heels variety at that; for after know-ing the young lady exactly one hour, the lad procured a dictionary and spelled out an ardent "I love you" with the best pronunciation possible in the circumstances. She confessed, through the same medium, a like feeling. But when he slowly and painfully hauled a "Will you marry me?" out of the dictionary, she rejected its dry offices and answered with arms and lips.

From the officers, who graced the wedding with their attendance in full regalia, I learned that, apart from the fact that the bride and groom could not speak to each other, all went merry as the prover-bial wedding bells. The pair were quite willing to pose for a snapshot. But the two pretty bridesmaids, who dressed up for a lark in sailor costume, made me promise most solemnly that their mothers should never see the paper the picture was published in.

The station, with its hangars and barracks, sits on the edge of a stone quay from where the big seaplanes take the water like giant fly-ing-fish. The neatness, order, and impression of a well-oiled machine running efficiently and without noise that I obtained at first sight, was largely explained by the fine team-work in evidence at the daily con-ference to which I was invited the morning after my arrival.

All the station officers attended. First the mail was read aloud, and each paper discussed before being handed over to the particular of-ficer under whose province it came. One communication revealed, at once, the sound democratic principles upon which our naval poli-cies are based and the interest its officers take in their men. It called for all enlisted men under twenty to be given an opportunity to take an examination for admittance to Annapolis, the best hundred to be appointed. Officers were instructed to afford candidates advice, assist-ance, and encouragement in preparing for the examination; and, judg-ing by the attitude of those present, I shall miss my guess if this station fails to place a couple of its Jackies among the lucky hundred. In fact, I found here the same good feeling between officers and men that had been so strongly in evidence on the destroyers I had cruised with—a loyal comradeship, friendly interest in each other, such as is not to be found in any foreign service.

A touch of unconscious humour sometimes cropped out—as when the commander commented upon the application of a man to be exchanged from a dirigible station. "He wants to be 'heavier than air.'"

The humour was conscious when, with a grin, he commented on

the last paper in the pile:

"I'm being sued for three dollars and sixty-five cents in the States; balance due on a golf bill"

Thereafter they took up the problem and necessities that had developed in the last twenty-four hours, which covered every phase of station life, from the bad behaviour of a certain plane to the health of the men. The report on the latter was excellent; for, like the Chinese medical system, your naval doctor is paid to keep the men well. The incumbent here was able to report a clean "sick-bay": this in spite of the fact that analysis of the town drinking water had shown one thousand colon *bacilli* per pint, not to mention an equal number of typhoid germs. Till a pure supply was finally obtained, every drop of water drunk at the station had been either chlorined or thoroughly boiled; and even now samples of the water were tested every week. So, anxious mothers whose sons are in the Navy, you may rest in the surety that Uncle Sam takes the best possible care of your sons' health.

Bombs and machine-guns, sights, ranges, bomb practices, tactics, convoys, and submarines bristled through the latter part of the talk.

Outside the sun was shedding a flood of golden light over the quaint old town. I could see through the window a fat windmill beckoning serenely for us to come out and enjoy the air. It was gristing its wheat as in the peaceful years that were past. It was all lovely, quiet, peaceful, the war seemed far off, till the commander began to read a report from another sector.

It set forth how two planes from that station had sighted a submarine on the surface the preceding day. While they manoeuvred to get between it and the sun to permit accurate sighting of their bombs, it submerged—a little late, however; for, sweeping low, the planes dropped all four of their bombs, scoring two direct hits. Like a wounded whale coming up from deep sounding with the harpoon still bedded in its vitals, the U-boat reappeared, its stern and conning-tower under water, bows pointing up at an angle of forty-five degrees. Evidently the imprisoned crew were making desperate efforts to right it, for the blind steel head raised and lowered and raised again from the frothing whirlpool churned up by the screws. Another bomb would have made a quick end, and, while one plane flew swiftly away to fetch more, the other hovered above the great steel creature's agony. It sank, but rose again—this time belly up like a dying fish, its port side exposed through its entire length. It sank, but rose still once again, this time with the other side exposed; but, in the terse language of the report: "In all that time the conning-tower failed to rise above the water."

It would be easy to dilate on the desperate mental agony of the crew battling for life amid the acid fumes of capsized battery tanks but of what profit? Sufficient that, after a last flurry, she rolled over and went down, carrying with her to the bottom a full complement of four officers and forty men. A couple of weeks before I had visited the *Lusitania* graveyard in a green churchyard in Ireland. Our consul there had shown me a picture of a great grave with its rows of tiny coffins; and, if I had felt disposed toward pity, the memory of the "Damn them!" that escaped his lips would have stifled the last compunction. They had reaped as they had sown.

A convoy had been reported as approaching our sector while we were in conference, and at its close the commander asked me, "Would you like to take a flight?"

Would I? A flight into the war zone guarding a convoy against the attacks of U-boats? *Would I?* Five minutes thereafter I emerged from his office, clad in a quilted, fur-lined flying suit and woollen boots, a full fledged aviator—as far as appearances go.

The planes were already launched, for they fly always in pairs, under strict orders never to lose sight of each other. With their golden fish bodies under the wide-stretched wings barred by two red-and-blue flying circles, they looked like gay aquatic birds. The sailor lad who filled the dual role of observer and wireless operator was already crouched in the cubby-hole in the bird's thick beak. Lest the wireless fail, however, we took with us a small basket of carrier-pigeons to bring back word of the ever-possible disaster.

Before the planes go out, of course, every wire and bolt is subjected to a microscopic scrutiny. The engine is tested and groomed to racing fitness. But bolts will loosen, wires chafe, and, falling into a propeller that whirls two thousand revolutions per minute, the tiniest nut will go through a blade like a bullet from a high-power rule. Or a loose wire will cut one like butter. In turn, the severed blade may cut off the tail and send the plane crashing down to complete wreck. But these possibilities belong to the game; hence the pigeons.

The messages are written on thin paper and stuffed into tiny capsules strapped to the pigeon's leg. Sometimes the birds pick them out—to provide against which, one inventive genius suggested that the carriers be crossed with parrots, with a view to delivering the messages orally.

The basket, with two pigeons, was stowed close to our feet. Just forward of the pilot's seat, where he could release them with a touch, two bombs hung in a bracket. That sounds easy. To hit the mark is quite another matter, involving calculations in which wind, velocity, and direction and the speed all have a place. When released, a bomb has, of course, the initial speed of the plane, and describes a flat curve through the air. Dropped from an altitude of seven thousand feet—for instance, from a plane speeding at seventy miles an hour—it will strike eighteen hundred feet beyond the point above which it was released. This fact accounts, by the way, for the poor shooting of the Boches in their attacks on London and Paris.

At the lower altitudes of from three to five hundred feet maintained by our patrol planes, the problem is simpler. The bomb may be let go from one to two hundred feet short of the mark. The sights, which work by triangulation, help greatly; but, even then, especially if a side wind is blowing, skill and good judgment are required to secure a hit. Accordingly, bomb-dropping with concrete substitutes on a pole the size of a periscope is frequently practised, with a remarkable average of hits. At one station I saw four bombs out of five hit the target, dropped at heights of from three to seven hundred feet.

The other plane, our escort, also carried a quick-firing swivel-gun that shoots a small explosive shell on her bows. She was already spinning around the harbour, warming up her engines, when we came out; and, while we followed suit, the officer pilot delivered a short lecture on the clocks that indicate levels, air pressure on the engine, propeller revolutions, and had me peep into the cubby-hole where the observer crouched over the wireless sender. After we rose, he would let down his aerial through a small hole in the bottom, whereafter we should be in constant communication with our base.

A deafening roar as the propellers increased their beat to two thousand a minute, a dash of smarting spray in the face, the sudden rise of a bitter wind that quite blinded me for the moment, marked our get-away. In a few seconds the great bird soared five hundred feet, then headed out to sea on a long sustained flight.

The day was cold in any case, and that fierce wind chilled to the bone the flesh of my face. Soon it settled into a more comfortable numbness. Then, as my eyes grew accustomed to the goggles, far beneath I saw a line of white surf lace stretching along seamed black rocks; a toy lighthouse in their midst; a golden beach. Beyond all a dull green plain scored with yellow roads that led through toy hamlets, past miniature windmills and churches. Very quickly all this vanished. There remained only the sun, gray-green through a golden haze, chased and fretted with tiny wavelets across which we raced our own shadow toward the indefinite horizon. I had always thought of gulls as flying swift and high. But down there a flock floated like bits of feather fluff, almost stationary in comparison with our flight.

Rising out of his cubby-hole, the observer now began to sweep the waters below with his binoculars, searching for submarines. From a plane the dark moving mass of a U-boat can be detected sixty feet under the water; and, though mere pinheads, mines are sometimes seen. Up there, with the roar of engine and propeller on one's ears, conversation is impossible. Though, for experiment, I shouted at the top of my voice, I could not hear myself.

Sign language obtains, and following the pilot's pointing finger, I presently saw, first, a fleet of red-sailed boats that fish in security under the protection of the patrols, then a large ship. From stem to stern she lay exposed to our gaze, just as though she were stretched on the sea below. The only sign of life was the shirt and underdrawers that fluttered horizontally in the breeze.

It seemed as if we had scarcely passed the ship before the island where we were to pick up our convoy hove in sight. To passing ships it no doubt appeared as a rock-ribbed shore smothered in surf. To us it represented the customary relief map on which a toy lighthouse posed with a toy hamlet, toy churches, toy windmills, all within the sea's edging of green and white lace.

The convoy, however, was not in sight. On the chance that it had gone up the other side—for the island must have been at least eight miles wide—we swept about it on a twenty-mile circle; and, as we came roaring down the opposite shore, there suddenly emerged from golden haze twenty vessels in three columns, with a destroyer in the lead and a converted yacht behind. We were still too high to distinguish human beings; but a white flash from the destroyer, followed by a quick electric blinking, was translated by the observer into a hearty greeting:

Hello, glad to see you.

The observer answered in kind. Then we flew on down the long lines of ships that rode the shining sea, each with a white feather astern, plumed above with smoke: first the destroyer, slender as a lance; next the broad, squat decks of a big tramp; on over ship after ship till the graceful shape of the converted yacht had passed beneath. Up there the sun shone with a golden effulgence unknown on earth. As it were in great silence—for that was the effect produced by the tremendous noise—we shot back and forth, circling and recircling the fleet. When we swung out on the flanks, it would break up to the eye into small detachments, to resolve once more into long, straight columns as we wheeled ahead or astern.

It was a beautiful as well as a wonderful sight, but when I tried to photograph it—well, imagine yourself standing up in a plane with an eighty-mile wind tearing at the camera while you strive to focus it on an object hundreds of feet below. Next time, sights will be fixed on my camera so that I can point it like a gun. Then I had to trust to luck and take a chance. Even when our consort obligingly sailed alongside and posed for her picture, it was impossible to locate her in the finder. The few pictures I obtained were a surprise to myself.

At intervals the observer had dived down into his cubby-hole, and we saw only his back above the wireless receiver. The interest that lad took in his work was fine to see. Always he was busy as a bee—now up, now down; swooping with his binoculars the sea below; signalling our consort or the destroyer; his face swollen and purple from the bite of the wind, but cheerful and happy as a soaring lark—a good average specimen of our fine sailor brood. He presently bobbed up, holding a slate on which he had chalked a radio just received. It was not from the convoy sailing so quietly under our shadow. It came hurtling down the meridians—perhaps from the Mediterranean, more likely from up the English Channel:

Enemy ships in sight.

With the German fleet bottled up in port? It seemed absurd. At the station, that night, the commander insisted that he must have misread the call. But I am not so sure of that, for the very next day the Paris papers came out with a description of a "tip and run raid" made by the Germans in the English Channel.

"Submarine quite near," a second ran.

This undoubtedly came from a distance. Nevertheless, the thrill of it tautened our nerves and stimulated our scrutiny of the waters for the forty miles we escorted the convoy across our sector.

A red pennant streaming below the golden fish belly of our consort gave the signal for home; and down the streaming path of the low sun, between blue sky and gray sea, we roared on like birds homing from afar. Once our pilot paused to circle an object that looked like a conning-tower and proved to be a barrel, and this gave our consort a lead of two miles. She was flying higher than were we, and, as I watched her against the sky, there came one of those incidents that gave rise to the rule that a seaplane must never fly alone. She wavered like a duck shot in midair—the next instant swooped down on a long nose-dive, and alighted with a great splash in the sea. She was sitting, when we came up, wings outstretched like a winded gull, thirty miles from home.

Twice we circled about her to make sure she was not in immediate need. Then we flew on, faster than the pigeons, faster than the swiftest bird, covering the thirty miles in a little more than twenty minutes, landing with barely enough gasoline left for ten more miles. Time had sped so quickly that I could hardly believe my eyes—we had made two hundred and fifty-seven miles in four hours and a quarter; a record for distance and duration for the station.

Going up I had felt anything but sure of my nerves. But the novelty, the stark beauty of it all up there, outsailing the birds between sun and sea, lifts one above fear. Excepting an occasional qualm when we careened sharply on a turn, I had not felt even nervous; and I learned later that these qualms were not without justification. A seaplane is altogether too heavy and stocky to do the stunts that a land machine does. So long as its speed keeps above forty-five miles and the engine runs true, it is as safe as a Ford 'bus on an empty road. But if the speed falls below that, or if she careens too steeply on a turn, she may go in to a "side" or "tail slip," turn turtle, and fall into the sea upside down.

I was, however, greatly tired and almost stone-deaf. Down here on the earth, it seemed so confoundedly quiet. The commander's greeting sounded like a run-down phonograph playing a badly cracked record several miles away. When he tried to talk to me, and I had to cup my hand to my ear and yell, "Say that again!" I fully realized the sufferings of the deaf. After this I shall be very tender with them—shout in their ears just as long as they care to listen.

"You'll sleep tonight," my officer pilot told me, saying goodbye. I did—like the proverbial log.

It was really he that most needed the rest. All the livelong afternoon he had held the plane in delicate balance against warring winds. Consciously and unconsciously, it must have been a terrible nerve strain. Yet now, instead of resting, he hopped from seaplane into motorboat, and went back to bring in our consort.

We learned, later, that she had a broken connecting-rod. Darkness fell before the rescuer covered half of the distance, and a strong tide carried the derelict six miles beyond the point at which we had left her. It was eight o'clock before the motor-boat caught the flash of the hand rockets her crew fired at intervals. Midnight passed before they towed her into the station. Her crew had been at sea for twelve hours with the mercury almost at freezing; yet the experience was light in comparison with that of another crew which had drifted for two days and nights before they were picked up.

We had neither seen nor captured a submarine that day. But prevention is better than cure. The daily sweeping of the French shore waters by our patrols has rid them of the nesting submarines that used to sow the channels with mines. It is human to love adventure. If it were not, where in the world would we get men to fly our aeroplanes? It is natural that these flying sailors of ours should long for the thrills of actual encounter. Instead of for bread, their daily prayer runs: "Give us this day a submarine." But the fewer they see the better. Their work will be just as valuable if they never see a single U-boat.

★★★★★★

Back again in Paris, I called on the executive heads of the service. They are clear-eyed sailor-men of large vision. They listened to my tale of what I had seen with the real interest your true creator always takes in the impression his work has made on a layman. Then they talked.

Till then my flight and visit had been an isolated experience; but now they fitted into a comprehensive scheme that covered the coasts of England, France, Italy, and Ireland. Already they had five thousand under their orders. The Naval Aviation estimates provided for seven thousand more, and just as quickly as the men and planes are provided for, the eighteen stations already established will be increased and extended till the trade routes in shore waters of these countries are completely protected. The station I visited, for instance, will have twenty-four planes when in full operation, working in pairs on two-hour patrols all day and on moonlight nights.

The French and English are watching with round eyes the tremendous war machine that Uncle Sam has called into being in such a short time. The *Genii* of the *Arabian Nights* have nothing on him. One wave of his long, brown, sinewy hand produces wonders beyond their magic. The French ports are crowded with our ships, troops, and trucks. The country is dotted with our aviation camps. In one naval

117

A SEA-PLANE SPINNING AROUND THE HARBOUR, WARMING UP HER ENGINES

TORPEDO BOAT DESTROYER AT FULL SPEED

station alone we have more planes and fliers than you could have found in all America before the war.

Go where you will, into the uttermost corners of France, and you meet our soldiers and sailors by the dozens, hundreds, thousands. They are everywhere, building railways, establishing motor transportation lines, in the forestry service, erecting gas plants whose product will make the Boches' best gas look like *eau de cologne*. But in all this mighty preparation there is nothing more vital than the Naval Aviation Service; for, in the last analysis, our participation depends entirely upon it and the destroyer service.

In the words of a song that was once sung in Congress, "*There's a great big hole in the bottom of the ocean.*" There is. It is so darned big that it will hold all of the supply-ships, transports, freighters, battleships, and cruisers that would soon be in it were we to pull the destroyers and planes off the U-boats for a few months.

Our destroyer fleet has made a fine record, but it still has to "sight the hare before it can hurt it." Just as military planes are "the eyes of the army," so the naval planes are the eyes of the destroyer fleets. Working together, the plane spotting from high the prey the destroyer cannot see, they are irresistible. The English realized this long ago. It is the thing these clear-eyed sailor-men in Paris are trying to bring about.

When the aerials of Admiral Sir David Beatty's flagship flutter in the breeze, four thousand ships begin to move. Yet, great as is this fleet, enormous its personnel, the English air service has twice as many men. An organization so large could never be a side issue. Accordingly, it has its own Minister of Aviation, governing his own department. Neither can we make naval aviation a side issue if we are to get the best out of it. It is too big, too important, a thing for that.

Our organization is splendid, as far as it goes. The ground personnel of the English aviation service—this includes officers' staffs—averages somewhere about seventeen men per plane. The French average is still higher. But our organization is being worked out on a basis of ten men to a plane.

This war has produced and killed off a large crop of prophets. Yet, after close study and personal observation of our air and sea forces, I have no hesitation in saying that the underseas war may be ended—if we want—in the next six months. To do it, all that is necessary is the greatest possible number of destroyers, planes, and men placed in the shortest possible time on the other side of the Atlantic. Send them over, and our skippers and aviators will do the rest.

CHAPTER 22

Flying Sailors: The "Lighter Than Airs"

"What the——" the commander began, as I stepped from the train, then concluded, "Who would have expected to see you down here?"

You see, we had crossed on the same transport five months before. "Down here" was a United States dirigible station on the south coast of France. Wherefore his surprise to see me, a civilian, there.

On the transport he had commanded a life-boat,—or would have had the U-boats gotten us,—and as I remembered his careful examination of its oars, sails, sea plugs; how he had tasted the water and biscuit to make sure they were fresh; also his lecture to the boat's complement of passengers; I knew that the station was in good hands.

While we were being whirled away in a "peaceful Henry," I took stock of his sartorial aspects, which had changed somewhat since we parted at Liverpool. A sailor on horseback has from time immemorial been something of a joke. A sailor on skates, roller or ice, wide trousers flapping like raven's wings in rhythm with his stroke, is hardly less funny. Neither does your seaman look well at the wheel of a buggy—horse or baby. In fact, it is quite hard to fit him into any background but that of the sea. His clothes and sea-roll clash with all other schemes. But, in their brown service uniforms, these flying sailors of ours are quite natty. But for the blue and gold shoulder straps, it were hard to tell the commander from an officer of the line.

Like the "heavier than airs" I had visited at another station, the war had dumped this lot of sailor lads in queer quarters. Beyond the dead flat mile of the flying field, a river—a real one, wide, deep, and swift, quite unlike the Thames and other creeks they dignify with the title across the British Channel—swept the stone skirts of a quaint, peaked

French town. Here and there, low stone farmsteads splashed the dull winter green of the prospect with blobs of white. An impressionistic painter would have used up half a tube on each. As in all south-France views, fat-bellied windmills waved gray wooden arms in the distance like plethoric millers warming their hands on a frosty morning. From the dead centre of all, the great canvas hangar raised its hundred feet of height and ran like an overgrown haystack three hundred yards along the field.

The men were at dinner when we arrived, in one of the low huts that form their home in this far-off land; and one glance at the table con-firmed an impression I had gained while cruising with our destroyer fleet—that the American officer, taking it by and large, does not "eat" as well as his men. Outside the day was gray and cheerless. A damp, cold wind blew over the bleak countryside. The commander had already told me the little French town nearby offered nothing in the way of amusement, not even a picture house. One could scarcely imagine a duller place to spend the winter months. But the lads had just been made happy by the arrival of a consignment of baseball and boxing sets, footballs, and a box of quoits, and were looking forward to the arrival of a Victrola and piano that were said to be on the way.

"When they come we'll be able to dance and sing in the evenings," one lad assured me with cheery optimism. "Then we'll feel all right."

"Sure we will!" another added. "And if they put us on the American Y. M. C. A. amusement circuit, we'll be happy as sand larks." And they will—that is, as happy as they can be away from Dakota or Iowa, Kansas, Alabama, California, or whatever State they happen to hail from. For the lauded beauties of southern France—human and landscape—cannot shake their allegiance to the girls and fair stretches of the motherland.

"This isn't so bad—for a while," one youngster summed it. "But after the war is over—me for the good old United States."

At the officers' table at lunch, I got a reflex of this happiness in the satisfaction all showed at the arrival of the outfits; for it seemed that a previous consignment of boxing gloves and bats had been diverted by a U-boat to the bottom of the sea. What an assortment of goods, by the way, has been opened lately for the inspection of mermen and mermaids! They must feel grateful to Fritz—at least, it is to be hoped so, for they are the only friends he has.

Of the dozen officers at the station, nearly all had trained at the dirigible school in Akron, Ohio. Many of them had been there together;

and from their small nucleus had sprung this big organization which would soon be flying four large ships. One or two of them had come out of civilian life in the last six months. I believe the commander and his lieutenant—who had also crossed on the same boat with us—were the only Annapolis men. But what the others had lacked in service they more than made up in enthusiasm. They had plunged head over heels into their work; were so thoroughly permeated that, so to speak, it seeped from every pore. Their conversation at table bristled with technical terms, was dark with flying lore.

"Sondage," "angles of inclination," "ascensional forces," "stabilizers" and "elevators," "fins"—full-mouthed phrases such as these confounded my layman's ignorance. I wanted to learn—and I did; among other things, that a dirigible is operated on practically the same principles as a submarine; which might be expected, as air and water, the mediums they float in, differ only in density. Both are fitted with narrow vertical and lateral planes, the "fins" and "stabilizers," which cut the air or water sharply and deliver it in a steady stream to the rudder and "elevators." The latter are large disks placed at the ends of the "stabilizers," and are really lateral rudders. Raised, they catch the wind and send the ship up. Depressed, they pull her down. The ship swings, of course, like any sea vessel in the direction the vertical rudder turns.

Dirigibles are safer than seaplanes, which fall if their motors fail; but the former can float for hours while their mechanics make engine adjustments or minor repairs. Also they can remain poised above a certain spot to deliver an attack or take an observation. The greatest advantage of all—they can stay out for thirty or forty hours and cruise seven or eight hundred miles. Because of these advantages, your "lighter than airs" are inclined to put on a little "swank" and look down on the "heavier than airs" as belonging to a primitive craft practically representing the stone age in flying. They seemed to be in doubt, however, as to their position in the scale with the submarine till the commander summed up a heated argument.

We steer by landmarks over the earth, by compass at sea. It isn't necessary to learn navigation. Those submarine chaps have to know a lot more than we.

Among the things the "lighter than air" must know is how to make the hydrogen gas he uses in flying. After dinner we went round to the gas-house where the hydrogen is stored in a canvas ometer which, in turn, is connected by canvas tubes with the dirigible ballonets so that the exact pressure required is always maintained.

Three "caustic" pits, from which the gas is evolved, still lay wide open on the outside as the French had left them, extending a cordial invitation to unwary persons. One of our lads accepted it one dark evening. Fortunately, he fell into a solution weak in comparison with the thick turgid acid in the next pit. Instead of being cooked to a crisp, he escaped with minor burns.

"Sondage" and "angles of inclination," those mysterious terms, explained themselves when the lieutenant, who was showing me around the station, sent up some toy balloons to determine the wind velocity. If they rise a thousand feet vertically while travelling the same distance horizontally, the wind is stronger, of course, than if they had risen twice the height. Worked by a scale through triangulation, wind velocity is easily determined.

"Come along!" The commander cut off the lieutenant's explanation. "We are going to bring her out!"

"Her" was the dirigible, now due to depart on patrol. The crew of a hundred and fifty men required to handle her were already in the hangar. With its long rows of latticed steel piers rising in a graceful arch overhead like fluted columns, its vast interior spaces, the golden light that suffused in mellow streams through the canvas roof, it looked like a great cathedral, and within it, like Mahomet's coffin, which is said to hang in midair without support, the great ship floated light as thistledown under the arch.

Your true sailor is as neat as a New England housewife, and just as crazy about brass and paint, and the ship's crew of mechanics were giving her the last loving touches. Every bit of brass, copper, and aluminium shone like silver or gold. The painted body gleamed like a grand piano. With glue and sandpaper, the master mechanic was touching up a slight abrasion on the propeller; for, with the blades revolving two thousand to the minute, the slightest roughness, will cause vibration, which will grow worse and worse till it finally wrecks the engine. An object as small and soft as a chestnut has been known, to pierce a blade like a high-power bullet and break it off through the ensuing vibration. Accordingly, as with the seaplanes described in the preceding chapter, every wire, nut, and bolt had been subjected to microscopic examination.

On the ship's bows she carried a Lewis gun on a swivel that permitted almost perpendicular depression; and, peeping underneath, I saw in their racks on each side the four bombs she carries for the especial benefit of U-boats. Today she was also carrying practice bombs made of concrete, which she would presently drop on a target.

The sand-bags and mooring-ropes having been cast off, the crew marched her out and round on a wide circle into the centre of the flying-field.

"Let her rise!" The commander gave the word from his station in the bows.

They slackened the ropes and gave her a few feet.

"Lower!"

They pulled her down again. She had floated in perfect balance with just enough buoyancy to carry her up to cruising height. A pull at a lever would release water ballast and send her higher in an emergency. But she rises and lowers for ordinary cruising by the power of her engines driving the "elevators" into the wind.

"Port engine! Starboard engine!"

They both went off with a puff of black smoke.

Satisfied with their even purring, the commander gave the final word: "Let her go!"

Simultaneously a dozen ropes slipped through the rings of her permanent stays. Then, slowly but with increasing speed, she rose and moved off on a wide circle that presently brought her heading back down the centre of the field.

In the meantime we had all moved back from the whitewashed lines that marked the deck of a submarine. At her height, nearly seven hundred feet, it could not have appeared any larger than a turtle's back. A bomb, too, has the initial speed of a ship when released; describes a flat curve as it falls; may be deflected by a side wind. The commander said, afterward, that he shot them two hundred feet short of the mark.

While it was falling, the bomb looked astonishingly large. A dead shot could easily explode one in midair. At first it just tumbled, turning over and over; then, as the wooden arrow feathers caught the wind, it righted and shot true to the target.

The ship had passed a hundred yards before it struck, well away from the concussion blast of a real bomb. Now she described another circle, came back, and dropped a second, third, and fourth. All but the last struck square on the target; the wind carried it a few inches to one side. But, though technically a miss, it would still have damaged a submarine. While the French had the station, they sank two U-boats; and, judging from that day's practice, our lads can be depended upon

125

AMERICAN DIRIGIBLE

The type now (1918) being used by the Aviation Department for hunting out U-boats

GUN MOUNTED ON THE CARRIAGE OF AMERICAN
DIRIGIBLE USED FOR DESTROYING SUBMARINES

to carry on the good work.

Each time she had come down the field, the ship's great hulk had cloven the air with a sough like a rising wind. On the last round she was going at a pace that put her in a few minutes low down on the horizon; but, just before she went out of sight, she passed a second speck that grew and enlarged almost as quickly as she had diminished.

"It's the V——! from B——!"

The lieutenant's face could not have lit up more brightly had it been his best girl instead of the second ship of the four that would make up the complement of the station. He added as she dipped her nose to alight: "If that's little D— at the wheel, you are in luck. He's the boy that can give you real stories."

It was, and he did as we two sat with him at a late luncheon. A small, dark-eyed Frenchman, he spoke English so perfectly that his narrative lost nothing in matter or spirit by translation.

"*Oui, M'sieu,*" he confirmed the lieutenant's assertion. "We sank two submarines at this station. With another we fought an artillery duel. *Oui!* The little V—— outfought a Boche U-boat with only her little pop-gun.

"We had sighted her steaming on the surface, and had she kept her course we could easily have come down the wind and bombed her as we passed. But she was wise, that U-boat—wise as a woman, who, as you know, is wise without knowing it. Instead of waiting for us, the U-boat headed into the wind, which blew so strongly that with our engines at their best we could make only fourteen kilometres the hour. That was the U-boat's speed, and while we hung astern, she fired fifteen shells at us. Some burst close—so close that the little V—— still bears the scars on her body. But, luckily for us and her, they did not set her on fire. We answered, and hit her, too. But our little one-pound shells glanced from her curve like peas from a bald man's pate.

"It was suicide to persist, so we struck a wide tack across the wind to outsail and come back at her from the other side, with the sun in the eyes of her gunners. But when we came about, she was gone, that U-boat; submerged and fled from our little V—— . But such is your Boche. A cunning coward unless the odds are his."

I took another look at that little Frenchman—he had spoken so quietly, as though hanging on the tail of a submarine, a mark for its gunners, was all in the day's work. He could not have been more than five feet high. He probably weighed in the neighbourhood of a hundred and ten pounds. But the spirit that looked out of his dark eyes was big as Mont Blanc. The soul of him could not be weighed in tons. He shrugged when I mentioned the danger.

"Is war ever safe, *M'sieu?* We do not always escape. Out there"—a fling of his thumb indicated the flying-field—"we watched the Admiral—fly off on a far mission. The plane was seen here and there and yonder, flying south over the land. A ship reported her well along the Mediterranean, a gallant sight between the sunlit sky and deep blue sea. Then"—his shoulders rose to his hair—"she vanished. Perhaps a submarine got her with an incendiary shell? A flash of flame between sea and sky, the splash of her charred body in the water, it would be over! Or she may have been brought down. It is perhaps that someday her crew will come back to us from an interior German prison."

Just as he said, a dirigible offers an immense target, but just how large I did not realize until, late in the afternoon, our ship came sliding out of the sunset's gold. The huge bulk of her, shining and ethereal, looked as big as the hangar.

While she was still a fly-speck on the red face of the sun, the lone sentry away up on top of the hangar had sounded the bugle blast that brought the men from the huts, a swarm of black bees. As she slowed and dipped down with engines cut off, the quarter-mile trail rope thudded on the ground. It was seized by a hundred hands and quickly bent to a "dead man" anchor. The guy-ropes were as quickly slipped through the stay rings, then, on a wide circle, they marched her around to the hangar.

She loomed larger than ever, going in—"some target," as the boys would say, for the U-boat they are going to flush one of these days. Personally, I hope they catch them under water—at least before they can unship their guns. But these flying sailors of ours show no mental disturbance at the thought of a give-and-take duel. On the contrary, like the "heavier than airs" I had flown with, the "daily bread" in their prayer has been changed to "submarine." They will get it, too—let us hope, in the slang sense of the term.

Meanwhile, they are carrying on. Daily they go forth on the patrols, escorting convoys up the coast, keeping the U-boats out of the French ship channels. Also they are making the best of a rather cheerless existence.

My last view of the station, going away, showed a couple of lads hammering the tar out of each other and the new boxing gloves under the lea of a bunkhouse. Farther away, two officers were breaking in the football with vigorous punts. The "heavier than airs" at the next station are all Harvard men. These "lighter than airs" hail from Yale. It won't be long till they are at each other's throats.

Still farther off, out in the centre of the flying-field, two games of baseball were in full swing under the wondering observation of a group of wooden-shoed French peasants. The cheery yells of the players followed me down the road.

CHAPTER 23

Flying Sailors in the War Zone

We sat on the edge of the stone quay, the chief pilot and I, dangling our legs above a miniature gale raised by the propellers of a seaplane that was being "tuned up." A dozen stout men were restraining the great bird from flight, and its attempts to break their grip strongly reminded me of a Christmas turkey in sight of the axe and block.

Two other hydroplanes and three small fighting-machines were also poised like yellow dragon-flies with attendant wasps along the quay. A machine-gun in one was being aligned, and its crackling fire at a sand-bag target, rapid as the reverberation of torn canvas, split the hum and roar of motors and propellers.

Such sights and sounds are to be seen and heard, these days, at any of the naval aviation stations Uncle Sam has scattered with a free hand along the cost of France. A nest of British gunboats, the night patrol, cuddled like sleepy ducklings under the opposite quay. Two squat monitors, bulldogs of the ocean, drowsed heavily farther down the channel—with their fifteen-inch guns, however, still trained on the German naval base fifteen miles away, in readiness for anything Fritz might start.

Behind us the little port town lay in the sun, battered and mangled by three years of war. A single monster shell fired from twenty miles away had laid its greatest pride, a fine old church, in ruins. Blank windows stared from deserted houses like sightless eyes of the dead. All were torn by shell and shrapnel: for in one hour of one night the Boche dropped ninety bombs in a limited area, and this was a sample of his doing.

The shells from that monster gun twenty miles away are, however, more feared by the townspeople than the bombs. When one crosses the Belgian trenches a signal is flashed to a sentry on a lofty

131

watch tower that dates back to the thirteenth century, but has not seen in six centuries of turbulence worse times than these. The sentry, in turn, sounds "Mournful Mary," a siren with a sob in her voice. From the other end of the town the "Old Man" answers in *basso profundo*. Whereafter the population has just seventy seconds to duck into the dugout while the great shell is tearing through the air.

The watchman's job, by the way, is no sinecure. A Boche airman emptied his *mitrailleuse* into the last incumbent as he flashed past one night. Neither has the American naval station escaped scot-free. Four bombs had struck within a few hundred feet of where we sat. All of which, the battered town, patrol-boats, monitors, formed a grim war background for the sea and land planes that whirred and whined above.

A tearing burst of machine-gun fire drew our eyes up to five British aeroplanes that were swinging and diving—fleeing across the sky in the war game. Three were in swift pursuit of two, but just as they gained to position the two looped the loop and dropped on their puruers' tails with a burst of blank fire. It was fascinating to watch. The chief pilot spoke, his pointing finger indicating a dozen white specks at least fourteen thousand feet up in the blue:

That's the British bombing squadron returning from a raid. They are big fellows that can do better than one hundred and twenty miles an hour with a heavy load of bombs. Those chaps evidently made a big killing, for when the luck is poor they fly low and drop quietly into camp.

From that awful height just then the planes began to drop earthward in a series of dizzy loops.

"There they go—pulling the joy-stick to beat the band! They must have cleaned up the German submarine base.

"There's no getting away from it—the British have set us a terrific pace. We'll have to go some to catch up.

"Come along, now, and I'll show you what we are doing."

As we walked here and there, peeping into huts, workshops, and hangars, the signs of war were everywhere. Not a building that failed to show scars and gashes from shrapnel and bombs. A table at which a dozen men had been sitting a few minutes before the raid was deeply scored by a splinter throughout its length. Yet, while practically under fire, with the additional handicap of building the station while training their men and establishing patrols, officers and men were straining every nerve to take the "British pace."

"So far Fritz hasn't bothered us much," the chief pilot explained. "But we are not allowing him to lull us to sleep. He'll wait till he thinks we feel secure, then he'll come sweeping out from the land to try and get us. But each of our seaplanes has a machine-gun mounted fore and aft, and three swift battle-planes go up with each patrol, so we expect to give a good account of ourselves."

The glint in his eye said a good deal more, for he was a quiet chap, who bore himself with that courteous mixture of frankness and reserve which is the hall-mark of the American university. Only by accident had I discovered that he had come into our naval service with another American from the Lafayette Escadrille[1] and had been cited by both the French and Belgian governments for shooting down German planes.

I had had great difficulty in getting him to tell of these exploits. He had been lucky in getting in the first burst of fire. The observer had collapsed. The pilot had crumpled and slid sideways, held in his seat by the straps. The plane had dived, spinning, to the earth ten thousand feet below. That was about all I could get out of him. But he was quite ready to talk about the others. It was from him I heard of how young H——, another American flyer, had chased a Boche aviator back to his hangar behind the German lines, and shot him as he climbed down from his plane.

"But that wasn't good flying," he commented upon the feat. "They got him next time he tried it. The thing I try to impress on our boys is to inflict the greatest possible damage on the enemy without cutting off their get-away. One live aviator is worth more to us than seven dead heroes. Fritz prefers them that way—heroic and dead."

The station had already given two names to the "roll of honour," for an ensign and a blue-jacket observer had fatally "crashed" the preceding week. But that is the inevitable price of war flying, and it had not affected the morale of the others. For the matter of that, each and all had had their narrow shaves. One pilot had saved himself by throwing the machine over on one wing just before he crashed, so that it absorbed the shock. The other Lafayette man had driven a plane at a hundred miles an hour between two trees twelve feet apart. He stripped both wings and landed with the motor in the bushy top of a pine a hundred feet farther on. Whence he climbed down and walked back to his hangar.

---

1. *The Story of the Lafayette Escadrille* by Georges Thenault also published by Leonaur.

He it was that told me of one plane, the finest and latest of the British makes, that travelled in perfect balance for one hundred and twenty miles after its pilot had been shot dead. Like a faithful carrier-pigeon, it flew till the last drop of petrol gave out, and it descended to a perfect landing in a level field with the dead man's hands still gripping the control.

In fact, all flyers expect a percentage of mishaps. Only two days before one of the little fighters had crashed into the sea on the other side of the British Channel and sank, leaving the pilot swimming for dear life. The seaplane he was guarding swooped down from four thousand feet and picked him up when almost exhausted, but the accident furnished one of those minor tragedies which birds and beasts contribute to the war. The carrier-pigeons that go with every plane to bring back the news of a breakdown had both been drowned. Nor was that all. Under its load of four men the hydroplane also broke down and had to descend. One of its pigeons flew straight home with the news, but the other fell in by the way with a boy and a "beebe" gun. After lying up in dock somewhere two days for repairs, the faithful little bird flew home, with its tail feathers shot off and a pellet wound in its back.

But there's the most curious case of all.

It was a yellow dog of the variety one sees quite often being huddled and made much of by small urchins on American streets. His air was cheerful as he nosed around for bones or anything else eatable the canine gods might provide, but suddenly he paused and shrank down in a queer, paralytic crouch.

"Shell-shocked," the pilot said. "He'll probably recover in time. Meanwhile he has learned his lesson. He bolts like a scared rabbit for the dugout with the men at 'Mournful Mary's' first yell."

We were standing then at the door of the first dugout; and for the comfort of mothers and fathers, sisters and wives of the lads here in the war zone, I can certify that everything posible had been done to make them bombproof. First a corrugated iron arch is bedded in thick concrete ten feet underground. Next comes an air space to absorb shock. Then a second thick layer of concrete surfaced with granite blocks that have proved their worth in resisting high explosives. Finally layers of sand-bags rise ten feet over all, topped with a glancing roof of thick boiler-plate. The doorways at each end are heavily bulwarked with sand-bags and lead around right-angle passages down below.

As we entered the pilot switched on electric lights that revealed the corrugated iron roof, long and dark as the upper arch of a big sewer. A double bench ran down the centre. Single benches lined each side. In case the lighting system should be destroyed, ship lanterns with candles ready to light hung from the centre of the arch. Each of the three dugouts in the station accommodate a couple of hundred men, and already they have been used. For Uncle Sam is ever careful of his men. When the "Old Man" answers "Mary's" mournful yell, it is all hands for the dugout till the alarm be proved imaginary or real.

The sailors, whom the pilot had called to pose for a flashlight below, displayed more of curiosity than concern about the probable effects of a bomb.

"We don't know yet whether they'll stand up under a direct hit," one lad said with a grin, "but we're liable to find out. That's all in the game. What we don't like is being yanked out of bed every night by false alarms."

In real American sailor fashion they were hauling all the fun that was to be had out of the situation. Fritz and his frightfulness drew from them only sardonic humour. The instant we released them, the players went back to their baseball, while another group lounged on the sunny side of the dugout and played with three little tow-headed maids from the French barracks next door.

Their ages ranged from five to nine, and never have I seen three prettier or nicer children. Like the dog—and the cats, if our sailors are to be believed—they have learned to dive for the dugouts in their "nighties" with their blankets in their arms at any old hour of the night. Just now they were frolicking like small kittens with our lads; but when their faces settled I felt that the raids had marked them. Fear dwelt not far behind the bright blue eyes. But I do not think that they consciously dwelt on it, and between raids they have a good time. Not a box of candy or parcel of eatables comes to the station that they do not share. Apart from certain small stomach-aches induced by indiscriminate largesses, they are as content as other children with whom air raids loom as an indefinite terror in a far-off land.

"A German plane hovered over here taking photographs yesterday," the pilot told me as I said goodbye that evening. "We rather expect to get it tonight. Rumour has it we're going to be gassed."

I carried that interesting piece of information back to the top story of the hotel where I slept with only a few thin slats between me and the Boche. Being bombed is one thing; gassed—quite another. No respectable person likes the idea of being asphyxiated in his beauty sleep. I once helped to pull a couple of farmers who had blown out the gas out of a hotel bedroom. They looked horrid. Their appearance haunted my sleep. I was sure that I must look like them when awakened by "Mary's" wail in the middle of the night. Far away the "Old Man" was also cursing the Boche. But louder than either—at least so it seemed to me—rose the *grumph, grumph, grumph* of German planes.

There is no mistaking the sound—and they were directly above. I know that I must have presented an accurate reproduction of the Bairnsfather cartoon which represents a Tommy, hair an end, stretched out flat on "No Man's Land" under the glare of a star-shell. At least, that is how I felt. But they were not after me. Four hours later "Mary" warned us of their return—alas! the hands of their pilots red with the blood of women and children in London.

CHAPTER 24

Flying Sailors: The Fighters!

Most folks, soldiers or civilians, wax a bit nervous toward the end of the passage to England or France—a general feeling that was well expressed by a young Scotchwoman on our boat when reproached by a fellow countryman, the bath steward, for her cowardice in refusing the morning tub: "You can think what ye will—I simply will *not* be torpedoed in my bath!"

It goes then, without saying, that two things are etched with acid sharpness on our memories—to wit: first, the grim snake forms of the destroyer convoy zigzagging in the sea mists ahead; next, the seaplanes booming like giant wasps out from the land to guard the last and most dangerous lap of the convoy. Ethereal as butterflies in a green meadow, they come so easily, go so fleetly, circling and recircling the convoy. But, of the million and a half of souls who watched them during the last year, how many knew—and of the few who knew how many realized—the enormous travail in mental and physical labour, the experimentation, failures, "crashes," deaths, that lay behind the easy grace of those flights?

Later I was to see them, myself, poised like golden insects in the tawny African sunlight between the smiling seas and deep blue skies of the Mediterranean. They would come darting out of the gray blanket of mist along the French coast to sweep the ship channels for U-boats and mines. But, though I had even flown with them on convoy patrols, not till I stood the other day "on the concrete" of our largest English station, did I realize in full the size and efficiency of our naval aviation service.

Take a look, with me, at this single station—one of a score that Uncle Sam has scattered with a free hand up and down the coasts of Ireland, England, Italy, and France. A single station, with a personnel of more than a thousand men, representing all skilled crafts; all at work in a veritable hive of industry. Its camouflaged hangars, each hundreds of feet deep and wide, run continuously for a quarter of a mile along the concrete, which in turn lay its hundreds of feet of width between them and the inclined ways that lead down to the water. All were crammed with seaplanes and Liberty flying-boats; a score of the latter already set up, while twice as many more, still in their crates, were holding an overflow meeting all over one end of the concrete outside.

The crates, by the way, are so large that it required only the addition of a door and windows to turn one into a comfortable three-roomed house for the British *liaison* officer. One would never imagine that the contents of half a dozen go into a single boat. But when my glance passed to three completed machines that were "tuning up" nearby, I understood. It is really enormous; yet the perfect adaptation of its parts to their functions gives it easy, graceful lines that take from its size.

The strident purring of their engines supplied merely an undertone to the continuous drumming roar of a single Liberty motor that was testing out propellers. The latter, you see, are made out of many pieces cunningly dove-tailed and glued into a whole, which is far stronger than a solid stick. But, before men's lives can be trusted to them, it must be shown that the job is well done. Accordingly, at gradually increasing speed, the revolutions are worked up to a climax of sixteen hundred a minute. Twenty a second? At that speed the screaming blades disappeared without leaving even the customary blur in the air. The motor was functioning so quickly that the movement of its valves could only be discerned as a faint vibration—every quiver, however, a gasoline explosion. Only a good propeller can stand that strain. While I looked on, one flew away in a shower of splinters. Others developed faults. But those that were left could be depended upon to drive a Liberty boat to Helgoland.

This was my first view of the Liberty engine, and I marvelled that a motor so small—not much larger, indeed, than a Ford—should be able to develop such enormous power—to get which, in the old days, marine engineers had to fill the bowels of a ship with a mass of machinery. In the last year a liberal crop of lies had been sown in England and in France about this motor—by the Hun, no doubt. It had been thrown together overnight by a garrulous crew of automobile salesmen! Its carburettor wouldn't carburet; worked up to two thousand feet, then *poufed!* It had corns, bunions, sore throat, black measles, or the mechanical equivalents thereof! But seeing's believing! In view of these evil reports, it was fine to watch its smooth, steady running. Finer to hear that even, drumming roar. Finest of all to see the three great birds, all "tuned" and taut, bombs in their sockets, machine-guns grinning from their ports, wheeling on their great trucks down to the water to proceed on a reconnaissance patrol.

One by one, they slid down the runways; floated off their trucks; shot out on the wide estuary; then, as the motors warmed to the work, lifted in long, low flights. Bound the first two came, rising higher and higher, wide wings inclined to their graceful circling, till the last boat was up in the clear. Whereafter they headed out to sea in search of U-boats, Zeppelins, Hun seaplanes, floating mines, or newly sown fields, and anything else that might be at loose in the way of fight or information.

In addition to reconnaissance patrols, the station convoys ships and sends special planes to engage reported U-boats. Three other machines next flew off to escort a convoy across our sector. Later, a single boat winged away to find, and bomb if possible, a U-boat reported off our coast. Thus the one morning showed all three functions in operation.

After the last boat disappeared, I headed into the pilot's room in rear of a hangar, where naval history is to be learned in the making at first hand. It was really a remarkable gathering I found there; for, of the dozen pilots who sat talking and smoking, all had graduated from banks, stock-markets, law offices, mines, and the universities within a year. Because they were young and had no other vivid life experiences behind them, they all talked "shop." I had only to sit tight to hear just why "Bill crumpled his left wing yesterday," or how Tom came to take his famous nose dive into the mud of the estuary last week. When their own doings are in question, however, aviators shut up like scared clams. I shall not soon forget the mental anguish exhibited by the late Major Raoul Lufberry, our "ace of aces," when I tried to interview him one week before he was killed in France. Profiting by that experience, I egged the boy who happened to be sitting next to me to talk about his fellows.

"Zeppelins?" he repeated my question. "Yes, we run into them now and then—but not if they see us first. They're scared to death of a seaplane—run screaming for help the moment they spot us. Though you can't blame them," he added charitably. "It's no fun being roasted to death between the sea and the sun. Usually a Hun destroyer answers their calls. But if they happen to be a long way out we stand a fair chance. One was shot down in the sector south of here two days ago:

the second in a little over a month."

He went on, after a little gentle prodding:

"Captain ——, the British *attaché* here, followed a Zep two hundred and eight miles, almost in to Helgoland, not long ago. Two of us had started with him. But that was our unlucky day. We both developed engine trouble and had to descend. It was a shame, for the three of us would have nailed the Zep for fair. It was the greatest disappointment of my life. Just picture it to yourself—everything running smoothly, and you gaining on the shining silver mass of the Zeppelin bursting along in the clouds overhead. Then *pop! pop!* The motor starts missing, and you have to land. I'll never suffer again like I did when that Zep went over the horizon with P—— in pursuit.

"A stern chase, you know, is always a long one. They covered a hundred miles before P—— gained shooting distance. A Zep, too, can mount faster than a plane. When P—— drew close, the Hun would drop a bomb or any old thing of weight, then turn up his nose and go shooting aloft a thousand feet, leaving the plane to crawl slowly after. Still P—— carried on, shooting up at the fat silver belly. He fought for another hour, and turned back only because his petrol was running out. He had barely enough left to make back to the base."

This was a fair specimen of Zeppelin actions. Equally dramatic, though more one-sided, are the brushes with U-boats. An old saw tells us:

Catch your hare before you cook it!

In underseas warfare this might be amended:

See your hare before you catch it!

In this the seaplane excels; for an expanse of sea double that which can be seen from the deck of a destroyer is open to the aviator's view.

Time is the next vital factor,—the time required to overtake the U-boat hare after it is sighted,—and, swift as is the destroyer, the swiftest thing afloat, its highest speed is a tortoise crawl compared with the downward swoop of a plane. Even if the Hun spies it a couple of miles away, a seaplane can still reach him before he dives. Moreover, unless he goes very deep, he can be seen under water; or, if out of sight, can still be traced by the air bubbles that float up from his screws. Of course—but let the boy get on with his story:

We see more U-boats than Zeps. Of those reported off this sector, there are two probable sinkings, one we are sure of. The last happened to be mine, so I can give you it straight. We were on convoy duty, that morning, about twenty miles out. The weather was lovely. Flecks of mist draped the water in successive curtains, like the flies of a giant theatre seen from above. But, up where we were flying, sunshine like golden wine flooded the world between sun and sea. Perhaps Fritz came up to get a smell of that beautiful weather.

Anyway, looking down between the curtains, we saw him steaming slowly along the surface. At the sight of us he closed up like a startled clam and dived; but his periscope was still showing when we swooped down and dropped a bomb from five hundred feet. Though it did not actually strike him, the explosion wrecked him internally, so that he had to come up— unfortunately for him, right under the bows of a destroyer that had followed us hell-for-blazes and now waltzed right over him.

The other? Though we haven't received credit for it yet, we feel pretty certain we shall. The British Admiralty, you see, admits a sinking only on positive evidence, and our marker buoy was swept away before we could bring up any evidence. So far we have been unable to find it again.

His comment on the Admiralty practice was loyal and just:

One wouldn't want them to be easier; for the whole world knows, now, that anything given out by the British Admiralty is authentic.

The life at this station also carries a liberal seasoning of those misadventures that are easier to read about than endure. "His motor stalled," says our morning paper, "and the pilot descended a hundred and fifty miles out at sea." Then, accustomed as we have grown to judging aviation distances by flights, we make mental comment: "Oh, yes! about an hour and a half at ninety knots."

Now the rescue of wrecked crews has, on one or two occasions, been effected by flying-boats. When a small battle-plane of ours crashed off the coast of France, the seaplane consort it was guarding nose-dived four thousand feet, and picked up the pilot who was left swimming in the water. Another time, four men stood for nine hours on the tail of a slowly sinking plane, and were up to their necks in water when found by two flying-boats. By splitting the crew between them, the boats succeeded in rising, and, albeit flying heavily as gorged fish-hawks, still made their base.

As a rule, however, rescues have to be made by surface craft, and even a destroyer takes about six hours to travel a hundred and fifty miles—six hours in which wind and tide carry the small human atom farther and farther from his reported position out there on the wide gray seas—six hours in which a storm may blow up and wipe out the last trace of the wreck, or in which night may drop its black curtain. When all this is taken into consideration—and destroyers are not usually available—such mishaps become adventures in the fullest sense of the word.

Every possible disposition is made, of course, to minimize risks. Carrier-pigeons, for instance, go out with each plane to bring back word of disaster. That, too, sounds easy. If not killed by the crash, you just sit around and, smoke till the pigeon brings help. But even here the usual percentage of human error can be depended upon to creep in. Carriers must not be fed for twenty-four hours before a trip; otherwise they will not fly home—as one aviator found, to his cost, when sent out with a pair that had full crops. One of the pigeons was killed by the fall. When released, the other merely circled and lit on a wing-tip beyond reach. Language had no effect on the recalcitrant bird, and when the aviator tore a clock from the fuselage and threw it at him—his aim, alas! was too good. He knocked the bird into the water. Though he plunged in and rescued the poor thing from drowning, it was too badly wounded to fly. He and it floated four days and nights before being picked up.

Another instance out-movies the wildest movie melodrama; for, after crashing, the plane took fire and burned till only a wing-tip was left floating on the water. It would hold up only two, so the third man had to swim around while his fellows rested. By the time they were rescued six hours later—a hungry pigeon having done its duty—each had put in two hours of solid swimming practice.

Worse than either of these cases, however, was that of the aviator who floated four days and nights on a single pontoon broken from his plane by the crash. Four long days, and as many eternal nights, he floated in the North Sea, exposed to January sleet and snow and frost. When picked up, his face, feet, and hands were all frozen. The wonder of it is that he recovered and is flying again.

A still more interesting story comes from a more southerly station, where our naval aviators are training and fighting side by side with veteran English pilots. I give it almost as set down in the simple language of the report, without any embroidery to lessen its force:

We had been ordered to carry out a reconnaissance and hostile aircraft patrol. After we had flown up the beach for about quarter of an hour the squadron leader had to plane down to the water to repair a broken petrol pipe, and while we circled above him, five German planes came flying out of the land on a course that would soon bring them upon us.

Taking battle formation, we flew straight at them—a manoeuvre they evidently did not expect or enjoy, for they turned tail and ran, with us in full pursuit. The engineer and wireless men were to serve our guns in the cockpit astern. I was in the fore cockpit with one gun and four hundred rounds of ammunition. So, though the Huns were too fast for us and drew gradually away, I still had a chance to try out my gun at long range—with what success I cannot say, for the tracer smoke faded out half way.

It was up to us, of course, not to leave our comrade, who would have been shot to pieces down there on the water. Returning, we circled once more above him till the enemy plucked up courage for a second attack, then drove them off again. After a third attack, we saw a small scout-plane fly away at top speed— undoubtedly to bring reinforcements; for, as we gave chase to the others for the fourth time, the scout came back with ten more German planes. Instead of the original five, the four of us now had fifteen to fight.

It was heavy odds; but, swinging again into battle formation, we carried the war to them, steering straight for their centre. Feeling secure in their numbers, they met us squarely. Four rose to our level on the port side. Five swung to starboard. The others steered directly beneath us, shooting up as they passed.

"In a very few seconds the air was blue with, tracer smoke. I concentrated my fire on the four planes to port. There wasn't much time to look around, but as my glance followed them in passing, I saw out of the tail of my eye Lieutenant G—— in a stooping posture, one arm hanging down as though reaching for something, his head resting on the second pilot's seat. As I had seen him do that before, I thought nothing of it till, a little later, I saw that he was still in the same position. Looking closer, I then saw that his head was lying in a pool of blood, and realized with a shock that he had been shot.

From that moment I had no clear idea of our manoeuvring; only knew that we were making a running fight of it, surrounded by seven Hun planes that had cut us off from our formation. Seven to one! And they were not trying to keep away from us, either; would sail right in and turn loose a burst of fire at a hundred-yard range. Yet, somehow, we carried on for ten miles, and finally drove them off—not a bit too soon, either, for our port engine was popping badly. We also had to descend to repair a broken petrol pipe.

This fine lad sums the engagement thus: "It had lasted a full half hour, four against fifteen, at ranges of from one to two hundred yards. Our cowl and fuselage were simply riddled, and all our other machines were thoroughly shot up. Yet, without losing a plane, we had shot down two Germans—one falling out of control to a bad landing, the other side-slipping to a crash from two thousand feet. While the petrol pipe was being repaired, I attended to Lieutenant G——. His heart was still beating feebly, but a bullet probably explosive had passed through his head, tearing a gash two inches wide. Though we flew home swiftly and procured medical aid for him, it was hopeless."

Hopeless? Perhaps surgically, but not spiritually. The man had fought his fight and passed out, leaving in his end one of those fine examples that act as a lever to lift human existence out of the animal rut. As one young English officer put it in a letter to his mother, the night before he was killed:

Of what great value, after all, is forty years of life more or less in this disordered scheme of things? The longest life is but as the flitting of a bat in and out of the firelight, a flash in the pan of eternity. Here we live splendidly while it lasts.

Finely said!

But the star story is that which, because of its supreme daring, spread scareheads an inch high across every paper in the United States. For me it has special interest because I had flown once with the squadron to which Lieutenant E. G. Chamberlain, its principal, belongs. Therefore it would be quite easy to set the stage and work up atmosphere; but, as this young man's achievement rises far above the wildest flights of fiction, any attempt at adornment would de-feat its own purpose. The story cannot be told better than in his simple report, spiced as it is with unconscious, nonchalant humour. It is only necessary to add that on the preceding day he had already shot down two German planes.

> We left the ground about 9 a. m., and joined our bombers at ten, going over the Marne. Machine and anti-aircraft gun fire was quite heavy, but did not bother us much. Our bombers hit a train, which blew up and raised an awful stew. Then, as we started home, we were attacked by thirty enemy planes. A dog-fight followed, in which we lost three machines and the Hun three. A few miles farther on, forty Huns came at us again, two to one. An awful dog-fight followed, in which we lost two bombers and four fighters, to one Hun down. At this time a bullet partially disabled my engine, so that it alternately died and ran in spells. After it was over, two other fighters and my-self and a French bomber found ourselves separated, and went on together. Owing to the missing of the motor, I kept losing altitude, and was also kept busy trying to fix a jammed gun. But it wouldn't fix, and I had only one hundred shots left for my other gun. About eight miles from our line, the firing of the anti-aircraft guns suddenly ceased. I knew what that meant, and, looking up, saw a circus of twelve Huns circling above my two companions above. Another was coming straight at me. Though my engine was still missing badly, I went straight at him like I meant it, fired, and he pitched straight to the ground.

One!
Having disposed of his enemy, and with the French bomber under his protection, Chamberlain would have been perfectly justified in flying on home. But listen:

> Just then my engine came alive again, and I started up to join the 'buzzards' dance of death above. The Huns were slowly tightening their circle around my two friends, who were dart-ing to and fro, and high over all the Hun leader sat waiting for someone to slaughter. None of them saw me climbing up into the hazy sun till I dove vertically at two that were going for Captain L——, and got the first with twenty out of my hun-dred rounds.

Two!

> He blew up and went down in blazing pieces. The second turned squarely in front of me just then, and I got him with

twenty-five rounds at thirty yards. He spun in flames, and the pilot jumped out.

Three!

My engine now began missing again. I looked around, and saw five Huns, including the leader in a gray-yellow Albatross, coming straight for me. Also I saw Captain L—— and Lieutenant H——. each down a Hun machine one falling in flames, the other minus a wing. Then my engine stopped altogether, with the Huns coming at me in pairs.

Five Huns coming at him in pairs and his engine dead? Somewhat of a situation! See how he met it, calling to his aid every dodge and acrobatic stunt he had learned on the training fields:

I dove vertical, then pulled into a loop without power, kicked into a vertical side-slip at the top, then saw an enemy plane directly beneath me desperately manoeuvring for a get-away. I got him, and down he went with a dropping wing on a fantastic spin.

Four!

I then went for the leader. He pulled a wonderful wing, but I had the idea first. We met head on, and he got my last thirty rounds where it would do most good. Down he went on his back, his body hanging half out of the machine, evidently hit himself. I turned, desperate, with no more shots left, and saw my two companions coming after the three remaining Huns— who, however, had had enough. They made off in wide circles.

Five! To which have to be added the two shot down the preceding day—seven in eighteen hours. Some bag! The young man pithily sums the results:

| Odds: | 12 enemy aircraft to: | 3 Allies. |
| Score: | 7 Huns down. | 0 Allies. |

Surely this was enough for one day. It proved, however, to be merely the beginning of a second series of remarkable adventures:

Going back my engine went bad again, and kept on getting worse. My companions, typical English soldiers, stayed with me until, near the lines, it cut out altogether and they could be no further use. In the meantime I had succeeded in fixing my other gun, and, seeing that I could not make the lines, I dove down on a troop of Hun soldiers that was coming up from the rear, and scattered them with machine-gun fire. Then I landed in a field of wheat about an eighth of a mile beyond their outposts. The enemy began at once to shell the machine, so I tried to set it on fire with my maps, but only succeeded in firing the wheat. The shells were now dropping close, so I crawled off into a wood, where I met three Huns. I was unarmed, but raised my compass to throw as though it were a grenade. One ran. Another fell, shot by his own fire. The third surrendered. I took his rifle and pistol, and ordered him on ahead. Soon we found a wounded French Colonial, and, picking him up, we carried him along to a French dressing-station inside the lines. Then I got to a telephone as quickly as I could and reported for duty.

The most remarkable thing about this astonishing story remains to be told. After shooting down seven planes, scattering a troop of Germans, taking one prisoner, and carrying a wounded man into the lines under fire, this modest fighter tried to hide the whole business—because, forsooth, having visited the British camp unofficially, he thought he might get into trouble for flying without his superior officer's permission. Fortunately, it was too big a thing to be hidden. Rumours of the exploit presently crept to headquarters. Whereafter his superiors showed good American common sense by calling for reports and recommending the young man both for immediate promotion and for the Congressional Medal.

Lastly, capping all, comes a small human touch. Achilles was vulnerable in his heel; a stomach-ache cost Napoleon the Battle of Waterloo; the worst "bad man" of the West I ever knew would run yelling at the sight of a bee. We are all afraid of something. And this young hero's comrades relate with great glee how, the Sunday preceding his exploit, he refused to go in swimming because he was afraid of the undertow. His bravery shines the brighter by contrast with this small weakness.

Surely we can be proud of these flying lads of ours—the prouder because they have forecast what we may expect when our flying organizations are complete and they go in deadly earnest after the Hun. But let us not be puffed up. England and France have lost in killed alone more than the entire American army at present in the field. We can profitably read, mark, and inwardly digest the headquarters' comment on the first of these two actions:

It gives a clear idea of the work our naval aviators are performing in conjunction with British aviators at the various stations to which they are assigned. Without exception, their conduct and performance of duty have been of the highest order, reflecting credit not only upon the U. S. Naval Aviation Service, but also upon the U. S. Naval Service in general. . . . Though this young officer conducted himself in a most gallant manner on this particular flight, he can scarcely be credited with having done more than the average day's work as performed by all of our naval aviators attached to the British sea-planes and operating on the war patrols.

It could not be better said. It is not given to all to shine. There are in some obscure stations far from the fighting zone aviators who will go forth on the daily patrols from now till the end of the war without even the stimulation of a U-boat chase. And this is the hardest duty of all—to pursue those sober paths that are never illumined by the lights of fame.

CHAPTER 25

A Flight in the War Zone

The patrol, two seaplanes and three fighters, were again perched like dragon-flies and wasps on the edge of the quay when I returned to the station next morning. The officer pilots and blue-jacket observers were already in their places—the former giving a last try-out to motors and controls, the latter clamping the "loads" on their machine-guns in the pits fore and aft of the pilot. The aft observer, by the way, needs to be cool-headed, for he has to shoot through a maze of wires and could easily cut off the tail.

The single aviators who fly the little war-planes were mounted and blinking along the sights of their guns, which shoot five hundred shots in one burst. It was war! In their leather helmets all looked like knights in hooded mail, and surely King Arthur's Knights of the Round Table never sallied forth on such desperate errands, for the fabulous winged dragons of their day have become real in this later age.

I also was to take a "hop"—not my first, but the others had been made on the south French coast escorting convoys with only an off chance of encountering a submarine. This was the war zone within shelling distance of the German lines! At any moment a squadron might come sweeping out from the land and cut us off! I had longed to go out with the British bombing squadron that had just flown in a great goose arrow across the sky, but this was hazardous enough. After the patrol had flown I dropped into the nostril of a third bird with a sigh of content.

This time my ears were wadded against the roar that had left me deaf for twenty-four hours on a previous trip, and I knew what to expect. I was ready for the blow of the wind in my face. I saw everything as we rushed down the channel past the nesting gunboats, squat monitors, lifting in the low, long flight of a mallard till we soared

149

high over the lighthouse at the pier-end. A wide circle laid the town directly beneath us, its red-roofed houses in vivid contrast to the dull winter green of surrounding plains, all bisected and cut up by gleaming water channels.

I did not half like it—there, over the land. A seaplane is a seaplane, and the ground looked so confoundedly hard. Those pretty red pebbles of houses would hurt like the dickens in the small of one's back. Though I knew we should crash just as violently if we fell into the water, still it *looked* soft. I was greatly relieved when the pilot headed out to sea.

A motor-boat had preceded us down the channel, and now lay with a couple of patrols, mere decks nailed flat to the blue sea. From a thousand feet we swooped down for a snapshot, then, shooting up again, he pilot laid a straight course down the coast.

As on my other flights, the coast lay below like a map in relief, hills mere green nubs amid winding channels; the beach a golden satin band edged by the foaming lace of the sea. Here and there a yellow road wound toward a distant toy hamlet. As before, the gulls floated far below, bits of white fluff against the green of the sea, stationary in comparison with the speed of our flight.

Today the visibility was not good; yet the haze that wrapped the sea and land as in a golden cloak lent them mystery. Anything might come out of that enchanted prospect—flying Boche dragons, for instance, belching five hundred bullets a minute from the midst of fire and smoke. But it was all so beautiful up there, the air so crystalline, sunlight golden clear, sea so wide and green, the Boche had no place in it. I quite forgot him. We roared on between sea and sky while the toy ships and little coast villages, with their maplike channels, locks, and long wharves, passed in swift procession beneath. I had almost forgotten I was flying, when—the motor stalled.

How quickly I remembered! For then it was that I recognized the truth of a clever British doctor's statement in the House of Commons: "Though the flyer may have no conscious fear, his nervous system is nevertheless afraid." Unconsciously my heart had synchronized with the motor. They stopped—and after the pilot had got the motor going again after falling a few hundred feet—they started again together.

We were then about twenty miles from our base, and, though we turned about at once, I cannot claim to any great enjoyment of the homeward flight. The way in which that pilot climbed for altitude was ominous and prophetic—for half way home the motor stalled again.

This time we had air room to fall in, and took full advantage thereof. After that—how that pilot did climb, climb, climb! But we needed it, for about two miles from home, at an altitude of seven thousand feet, the motor gave its last kick—refused us another turn.

Seven thousand feet in midair—and the motor stalled. A nice predicament for a peaceful correspondent! We fell at first, of course; then, as the planes took hold of the wind, the great bird steadied and swooped on down in a wide hawk spiral that carried us into and over the land.

It was a new sensation, that headlong dive through golden sunlit space in silence broken only by the harping of the wind on the wires. I should have enjoyed it—if I had not been quite so afraid.

I hope and believe the pilot did not notice my fright, for I camouflaged it with a few snapshots at those little red pebbles of houses as we fell. Perhaps he was as much afraid as I, though I do not think it. The pilot, whether of a plane or an automobile, has this advantage over the passenger—he knows what he and the machine are doing. In the pride of skill he no doubt took pleasure in the sickening careens on the curves that seemed to me the beginnings of the end.

But, be all this as it may, for six minutes we fell, fell, fell, and as each loop brought those miserable little houses up closer, I experienced again that absurd preference for the sea. I wished with all my soul that friend pilot would keep out over it.

The channel in front of the station, too, looked about the size of a cotton thread, and there was so much land on each side of it. Even at a thousand feet it looked no wider than a length of baby ribbon. I did not believe we could possibly hit it, and was rather surprised when we took the water with barely a splash almost in front of the hangars.

"It was one of the prettiest spirals I ever saw," the chief pilot congratulated us as we came ashore.

I do not doubt it, but—I should not care to do it again. Nevertheless I am glad to have had the experience, for it has deepened sincere admiration for our flyers. We used to be told that civilization had sapped the fighting spirit of the race—left it tame and degenerate. But one of the greatest lessons of this greatest of wars is—that the highest courage is born of the highest culture. Our universities have sent their best to the flying corps.

To the flyers, those fine lads of ours who go daily out to rid the seaways of the submarine, one cannot give their just due; it is beyond the power of language; for in the course of their every-day duty they face not only death but also dominate the profoundest fear of our race. The falling dreams of a child are an inheritance handed down the ages from the far time when our ancestors roosted in the tops of trees. The sleepy-heads among them fell and were killed. The timid, in whom the fear of falling persisted even in sleep, survived to reproduce their kind and fix the falling fear in the race.

And do not imagine that the flyer differs from the rest of us, is immune from fear. Of course he does not think about it—anymore than he can help. Nevertheless the English doctor already quoted spoke truly when he said that the flyer's nervous system is always afraid. A bad crash will sometimes bring that subconscious fear to the surface, and, if not, the strained nerves still give at last. One by one, the flyer sees his fellows go down to their end. He knows that the pitcher that goes to the well too often is bound to be broken. Yet, knowing it, he goes on flying.

And that, to me, is the great wonder of this war—that lads can be found by the thousands and hundreds of thousands in whom patriotic pride and manly courage dominate not only the fear of death, but also the most profound instinctive dread of the race. By the example they are leaving for future generations, they have made this war worthwhile.

CHAPTER 26

The Merchant Marine, the Prey of the U-Boats

"We are the prey, you know," the first mate observed. "The prey of the U-boat just as much as the deer is the prey of the tiger."

"That's right," the second mate confirmed. "Fritz is the hunter and we are the hunted."

We were enjoying the cool of evening on top of a building, centuries old, in a hot Mediterranean port. An arc light below our level shed a flood of light down into the narrow gorge of the street, transmuting its chrome-yellow walls into purest gold. The soldiers and sailors who had choked it an hour ago were now all gone—back to their barracks on the huge rock towering above us, or out to the ships dozing in darkness on the harbour's black bosom. There remained only a knot of Arabs, who made a wonderful blotch of colour in their flowing white *burnouses*, red *fez* caps above visages of polished copper.

From the peak of the rock a powerful searchlight stretched its slender white finger over the harbour, now lifting a ghost ship out of the night, again shooting straight out to sea in search of the ever-possible U-boat. A myriad insects danced in its white fire, ethereal sparks—each no doubt as concerned with its private affairs as we with ours; which happened to be the part played by the merchant marine in the underseas war.

It is, by the way, the "Senior Service"; for, very quietly, without any of that publicity which bathes the "Navy" with the limelight of fame, the merchant marine has gone quietly about its lawful—sometimes unlawful—occasions since the dawn of history, carrying the world's goods to and fro across the seas. In the course of these ordinary duties it found time to discover a few continents, and to seed them down thereafter with those hardy pioneers whose stock throve and multiplied into great nations; for from the Phoenicians to Amundsen, it has always been your merchant adventurer that placed the outlands upon the map. Through the generations he carried on, in the face of gales and typhoons, water-spouts, pirates, lee shores, usually ill fed, always hard driven, paying in addition a heavy toll of lost ships and drowned men for the privilege of doing his quiet, unmurmuring duty.

And when the greatest of wars broke out? Just as its forebears faced Kidd, Lafitte, and the Algerian, Malayan, and Chinese pirates, so the present generation put to sea unarmed this should never be forgotten—put to sea *unarmed*, in defiance of the U-boat, to maintain the trade routes and bring their daily bread to England and France.

But for their splendid heroism, the Allies must have been starved into submission; and, knowing this, the Hun did his damnedest, in the literal sense of the term, to frighten the merchant sailors off the sea, out-pirating the worst *buccaneer* that ever flew the skull and crossbones. The *Sink them without trace* of the German Ambassador to the Argentine is, indeed, the exact equivalent of Kidd's *Dead men tell no tales.* But murder will out. We know, now, that both anterior and subsequent to the discovery of that tell-tale cable, the U-boats were diligently practising his murderous precept; *for, since the beginning of the war, eighty-seven British vessels alone have disappeared "without trace."*

Eighty-seven without trace! What dark crimes are hidden behind that fact—not to mention the enormities perpetrated in open day! Four thousand seamen have been carried away to German prisons. *Fifteen thousand* more lie at the bottom of the sea. Yes, fifteen thousand of the finest men that the Allied and neutral countries ever sent to sea. Those that were left saw their vessels torpedoed, their mates blown to pieces. One man I know personally was blown up twice in one day—actually blown up into the air. Others have been "dipped"—as they call torpedoing in their careless sailor way—three or four times. One man holds the record with nine "dips," and, though quite profane, his confession of faith completely expresses the spirit of his fellows:

To hell with the U-boats! They can't keep me off the sea.

And they cannot. Though the Hun murdered them openly and secretly in cold blood, the merchant sailors continued to put to sea, unarmed and unafraid; for, from the beginning of the war, there is no record of a single seaman refusing through fear to sign on for another voyage.

Conduct such as theirs naturally tends to build up in one's mind an image of a Viking figure, brawny, breeze-blown, defiant, as representative of the merchant sailor. A modern artist would be more likely to choose for his model a half-naked stoker, begrimed with soot and sweat, misshapen and distorted by years of labour in the heated bowels of many ships. By sheer contrast, the heroism masquerading behind that rude figure would shine the brighter.

The two mates taking the cool with me up there on the roof would not fit into either type. Instead of the stern old sea-dogs of fiction, picture two slim English youths, nice looking, well spoken, delightfully courteous. The elder was only twenty-three, for many a good mate and master lie with the fifteen thousand at the bottom of the sea, and promotion comes rapidly, these days, to lads of parts. Both of their vessels had been torpedoed in the last week, but they were shipping again tomorrow.

The hoary elder had, indeed, been "dipped" three times before. The second mate could boast only two torpedoing in his, but made up for it by having been shot off the bridge of his ship in the course of a duel with a U-boat. His account of it unconsciously revealed that dogged, quiet, sheer pluck that animates the merchant marine:

> It was really uncanny, the way the first shell came dropping, as it were, out of the sky, for there wasn't a thing in sight. *Whoosh! Bang!* it exploded about a hundred yards away. Nearly a dozen had fallen around us before we picked up the conning-tower of the U-boat with our glasses about four miles astern. All the time they had dropped closer and closer till our decks were wet by the splash and strewn with shell splinters.
>
> We opened on him, then, with the stern gun, and during the four hours we fought him, he drew continually closer, and finally put a shell aboard us. After that he never missed. One dropped squarely on the stern gun, killing the pointer. The next carried away our wireless. Another exploded in the engine-room and brought us to a stop. After that I don't know much about it, for when I regained consciousness I was down on the fore-deck under the wrecked bridge with the ship's carpenter, who was trying to stop the bleeding from my arm.
>
> The shot had blown the helmsman to bits and tore off the captain's arm as he was throwing the books and papers overboard. But the poor old fellow never felt it, for a splinter had

pierced his heart. Our flag was down, and the U-boat had come alongside. To give the devil his due, this particular commander behaved well—gave us plenty of time to lower the boats, and even supplied bandages for the wounded.

"But don't imagine they are all like that," the first mate put in. "That very day another U-boat shelled the boats of the *Aguilar*, killing two women and two men."

The caution was not necessary. A son of mine, who is at sea on an American destroyer, had told me how his ship had towed into port a set of boats that were full of the shell-torn bodies of women and men. In those sombre records in which the British Admiralty sets down the crimes of the U-boat commanders, I had read of the *Falaba*, shelled with women and children aboard, with a loss of life of one hundred and four. Of the unfortunate crews of the *Middleton, Eavestone, Addah, Vanland*, one shell killed eight men of the *Addah*; wherafter the U-boat machine-gunned the survivors struggling in the water. The crew of the *Vanland* were machine-gunned in their boats.

The torpedoing of the *Harpalyce*, the *Euphrates*, and the *Lars Kruse*—Belgian Relief ships plainly marked as such and sailing under German safe conducts—forms part of that record. Seventeen men went down with the first; thirty-two out of thirty-three in the second; the third also had one survivor out of eighteen—all murdered while proceeding on an errand of mercy.

In another case, after offering to tow the boats to land, the U-boat suddenly submerged and drew the string of boats under, drowning all but two men out of fifty. Another string was saved only by the suspicion of a sailor in the first boat, who cut the tow-rope just as the U-boat dived. Varying this devilish cruelty, another Hun commander smashed the oars, threw the sails overboard, took away the emergency rations, and even filled the water-kegs with brine from the sea before turning the boats adrift a hundred and fifty miles from land. Fortunately, they were picked up two days later.

Even fishing-boats have not been spared. An earnest of what the deluded Sinn Feiners have to expect from their German sympathizers is supplied by the *Pretty Polly*, a fishing-smack that was proceeding on her lawful occasions one morning off the Irish coast. After placing on board a bomb that sent her, a twisted mass of wood and iron, to the bottom, the U-boat sailed away, leaving the men who were not killed by the explosion to drown far out at sea.

Everyone remembers the *Lusitania*, and the drowned babes that were taken from the locked arms of their dead mothers. Neither shall we soon forget the *Belgian Prince* and her crew, drowned on the deck of a submerging U-boat. Their cases stand boldly forth from the bloody welter that the Hun has made of the underseas war. The method employed with the *Belgian Prince*, moreover, sends a beam of light into the darkness that had previously shrouded the fate of those *eighty-seven ships which have disappeared without trace*. But for sheer cruelty, absolute barbarity, the case of the ill-fated *Maristone* out-Huns even those two famous cases.

Though I had read it already in the records, it took on a deeper blackness when related by the first mate, whose ship had picked up the solitary survivor:

> He was the ship's cook, and had been fifteen hours in the water. He was almost crazed by what he had seen and endured, and we had to pull the story out of him in bits. It seems that the explosion wrecked the boats so badly that eighteen of the crew were left swimming in the water when the ship went down. It would have been bad enough to have left them to drown. But, what was far worse, the U-boat sailed round and round them, her crew on deck, laughing and jeering at the cries and screams of the unfortunate sailors as they were seized and dragged down, one by one, by a school of sharks. It was to be another case of 'Sink without a trace'; or would have been but for the fact that the sharks were so gorged by repletion that the cook was left alive to tell the tale.

Unbelievable! your pacifist will exclaim. I would that all of his white-livered tribe might have heard the mate's summary and indictment:

> I have heard it urged, as partial excuse, that the U-boat commanders were acting under stern orders from the German High Command, but that is no excuse. Can you imagine a British or American officer carrying out orders to fire on boats containing non-combatant men, women, and children? He would face dismissal from the service first. Or, if an officer could be found to give such an order, do you think any English or American sailor would carry it out? He'd prefer to face a firing squad.
>
> It's no use to quibble or chop logic about it. The things these U-boat men have done have stamped them as naturally blood-

thirsty and cruel. From prince to peasant, they are all the same. By their own acts the German people has stamped itself as the most barbarous people on earth; and if we allow mawkish sentimentality to close our eyes to the fact when we come to the peace table, our descendants will someday curse us for it.

In view of all that has been done by the U-boat, it is comforting to know that it does not always have things its own way—even with lone merchantmen. Of the hundred and fifty or sixty U-boats that now lie at the bottom of the sea, a respectable number were sent there by fighting skippers of the merchant service. While the long finger of light above lifted and lowered, and swung, prodding here and there in the outer darkness, the first mate described an engagement a former ship of his had fought with a U-boat:

We had a narrow shave as a starter, for we actually split in between two torpedoes that passed twenty feet ahead and astern. That was enough to throw a cold chill into almost anybody, but it merely made our captain mad. A friend of his had spent three years in a Ger-man prison and come home all done in.

'If ever I get close enough to a U-boat,' I had heard him say again and again, 'it will have to pay Bill's account.'

So now, instead of running, he swung on the helm till he got the U-boat astern, then stopped the ship and let it come within easy range. I suppose they thought we'd surrendered, for they did not fire till we let fly with our after gun. Then they opened, returning two shots to our gun, for they had a gun mounted on each side of their conning-tower. Our first shot flew high, but the second and third landed. Out of thirteen shells we fired, eight were hits, and after the last a puff of smoke flew out of the U-boat hatches. She rolled over, stood on her head, went under, and reappeared with her stern in the air, then sank. 'Bill's account' was duly settled.

The story reminded the second mate of another fighting skipper:

Your old man was the same sort as Captain M———. He fought a night duel with two U-boats, one astern, the other to port. He had to fire at their gun flashes while steaming at full speed; but finally, after a long action, he landed a shell squarely on one U-boat and put it out of business. The other then quit the chase. Out of seventy shells fired at him, only one landed, killing the cook and ten sheep.

Followed stories of a sailing vessel, the only one on record, that outfought and sank a U-boat in a lively duel; of a steamer that fought a daylight battle with two U-boats and drove them off by her accurate fire; of another vessel the crew of which stood by and worked their stern gun till the water rose to their knees. When she sank, indeed, the gun-pointer walked down her port side as she heeled over to starboard, and stepped quietly off into the water. They told, too, of tricks by which Fritz scores on unwary ships. Of large brown sails hoisted, camouflaging the conning-tower so that it looks like a fishing-boat. Of mines floating beneath a foot or two of faked periscope, tempting vessels to ram. Of deeper treacheries where boatloads of survivors have been used as decoys to lure other vessels within easy torpedo shot. Of S.O.S. signals wirelessed from abandoned vessels behind which the U-boat lurks. Of periscopes sticking an inch above the gunwales of smashed boats. Of—of the whole bag of tricks, too foul to occur to any but a German mind.

Also they recited stories of hardship following disasters. A shipmate of the second mate, just a boy, was picked up, frozen fast to a plank on which he had floated for days in the North Sea. In return, I was able to tell them of that super-crew that stuck it out for five days and nights, persistently rebuilding their raft, while swimming in the water, every time it was smashed by a wave. Another crew was swept in their boats from the Bay of Biscay far out into the Atlantic in the frost and snow and gales of a stormy March. They had little water and few biscuits. Many were frost-bitten, and they died, one by one, till out of twenty-three only nine were left when picked up ten days later.

This welter of suffering and misery was illumined by saving flashes of human feeling. Men have stripped off their own clothing to keep women alive—only to die with them. There were many stories of men who died to save others, and tales of self-denial, long-suffering, patience, kindness so universal that it included even animals. Many a mascot has been given first place in a life-boat. When the solitary survivor of the *Belgian Prince* found the ship's cat floating on a piece of wreckage after he himself had been swimming for twenty hours, he stayed by and saved it.

Before the war we were not lacking in that type of philosopher whose habit it is to sit in judgement on the race and pronounce it degenerate. We were repeatedly assured that all of us were going to the bow-wows. But, stripping away the soft swaddlings of civilization, the great conflict revealed in us the primal virtues in larger measure than ever before. Among no class have they been exhibited to a greater degree than by the sailors of the merchant service. Though the Hun's barbarities have not stopped short of torture, as before said there is no record of a single sailor refusing to sign on for another voyage through fear. Neither has any seaman gone on strike—would that this might be said of some other trades!—to obtain either better conditions or more pay. Excepting the single instance when a British crew rightfully refused to take out a vessel in which pacifists had engaged passage to meet and shake hands with their German "comrades" at Stockholm, no ship has been delayed one minute by their action. From the beginning, the mercantile marine has played the game—will go on playing it to the end.

As beforesaid, but for the merchant sailor the Hun would have won the war by starving out England. Thanks to him, the Hun's threat to *bring England to her knees*—and by England he meant the whole world—was written on the waters, inscribed on the shifting sands. In the attempt to fulfil it, he piled cruelty on cruelty, frightfulness upon frightfulness, only to have them react upon himself. Like the dragon's teeth of the classic myth, the cruelties he sowed broadcast on land and sea sprang up against him in new armies of men. His infernal labours have brought him, in place of the comfort and ease he formerly enjoyed, nothing but loathing and contempt. A proscribed race, his sentence is to be read on the wall—henceforth to walk alone through an unfriendly world, an object of suspicion and contempt.

LEONAUR

ALSO FROM LEONAUR
AVAILABLE IN SOFTCOVER OR HARDCOVER WITH DUST JACKET

ESCAPE FROM THE FRENCH by *Edward Boys*—A Young Royal Navy Midshipman's Adventures During the Napoleonic War.

THE VOYAGE OF H.M.S. PANDORA by *Edward Edwards R. N. & George Hamilton, edited by Basil Thomson*—In Pursuit of the Mutineers of the Bounty in the South Seas—1790-1791.

MEDUSA by *J. B. Henry Savigny and Alexander Correard and Charlotte-Adélaïde Dard* —Narrative of a Voyage to Senegal in 1816 & The Sufferings of the Picard Family After the Shipwreck of the Medusa.

THE SEA WAR OF 1812 VOLUME 1 by *A. T. Mahan*—A History of the Maritime Conflict.

THE SEA WAR OF 1812 VOLUME 2 by *A. T. Mahan*—A History of the Maritime Conflict.

WETHERELL OF H. M. S. HUSSAR by *John Wetherell*—The Recollections of an Ordinary Seaman of the Royal Navy During the Napoleonic Wars.

THE NAVAL BRIGADE IN NATAL by *C. R. N. Burne*—With the Guns of H. M. S. Terrible & H. M. S. Tartar during the Boer War 1899-1900.

THE VOYAGE OF H. M. S. BOUNTY by *William Bligh*—The True Story of an 18th Century Voyage of Exploration and Mutiny.

SHIPWRECK! by *William Gilly*—The Royal Navy's Disasters at Sea 1793-1849.

KING'S CUTTERS AND SMUGGLERS: 1700-1855 by *E. Keble Chatterton*—A unique period of maritime history-from the beginning of the eighteenth to the middle of the nineteenth century when British seamen risked all to smuggle valuable goods from wool to tea and spirits from and to the Continent.

CONFEDERATE BLOCKADE RUNNER by *John Wilkinson*—The Personal Recollections of an Officer of the Confederate Navy.

NAVAL BATTLES OF THE NAPOLEONIC WARS by *W. H. Fitchett*—Cape St. Vincent, the Nile, Cadiz, Copenhagen, Trafalgar & Others.

PRISONERS OF THE RED DESERT by *R. S. Gwatkin-Williams*—The Adventures of the Crew of the Tara During the First World War.

U-BOAT WAR 1914-1918 by *James B. Connolly/Karl von Schenk*—Two Contrasting Accounts from Both Sides of the Conflict at Sea D uring the Great War.